TABLE OF CONTENTS

ACRONYMS

ANM	Arab Nationalists' Movement
BAED	British Army Element Dhofar
CENTCOM	Central Command
CSAF	Commander of SAF
CSOAF	Commander Sultan of Oman's Air Force
CSON	Commander Sultan of Oman's Navy
DAG	Democratic Army of Greece
DBS	Dhofar Benevolent Society
DF	Dhofar Force
DLA	Dhofar Liberation Army
DLF	Dhofar Liberation Front
DSO	Dhofar Soldier's Organization
EAM	Communist Party military wing
EAO	National Band of Greek
EDES	National Republic of Greek League or in Greek *Ethnikos Dimokratikos Ellinikos Syndesmos*
ELAS	Communist guerillas
FM	Field Manual
GCC	Gulf Cooperation Council
KKE	Greek Communist Party
MNF	Multi-National Force
NFR	Northern Front Regiment
NGO	Non Governmental Organization

PDRY	People's Democratic Republic of Yemen
PFLOAG	Peoples' Front for the Liberation of Occupied Arabian Gulf
PFLO	Peoples' Front for the Liberation of Oman
RAF	Royal Air Force
RHAF	Royal Hellenic Air Force
SAF	Sultan's Armed Forces
SAS	Special Air Service Regiment
SEK	Greek Socialist Party
SOAF	Sultan of Oman's Air Force
UNRRA	United Nations Relief and Rehabilitation Administration
USAF	United States Air Force
USAFE	United States Air Force Europe
USAGG	United States Army Group in Greece

ILLUSTRATIONS

CHAPTER 1

INTRODUCTION

This manual [FM 3-24] is designed to fill a doctrinal gap. It has been 20 years since the Army published a field manual devoted to counterinsurgency operations.

-- Lieutenant Generals David H. Petraeus and James F. Amos

The U.S. Army and U.S. Marine Corps, in an attempt to adapt to the current operational environments, have recently published a new counterinsurgency field manual. FM 3-24, *Counterinsurgency* is designed to give the American warfighter a doctrinal template to defeat insurgent threats we will face in the near future. General David Petraeus, the current commander of United States Central Command whose area of responsibility includes Iraq and Afghanistan, stated that the manual had filled a doctrinal gap since the previous manual had not been updated in 20 years. Does this latest addition or refinement to the Army's doctrine offer any great new insights on how to fight this type of war and does it stand the test of time when compared to previous counterinsurgencies in the modern era? Is the Army's leadership relearning similar principles that the men who have gone before them had learned or is the manual's approach that has recently shown success in Iraq radically different from successful approaches used in past counterinsurgencies? Such a simple and basic introductory statement from the central military figure in defeating the insurgencies in Iraq and Afghanistan sets both historians and strategists in motion to compare and contrast past and present conflicts involving similar situations.

FM 3-24, if not for its content then for its timeliness, could be the baseline of standard beliefs, principles and practices for counterinsurgency operations that leads the

1

United States Army and Marine Corps into the 21st century. By studying previous conflicts Soldiers and Marines can learn not absolutes, but exponential experience beyond their years which can serve as references and will help them place future missions in historical and cultural context. This in turn will help develop their situational understanding. This look into the past was intended, if not to find the silver bullet to fight counterinsurgency, at least to hone understanding about successful and unsuccessful practices in order to learn and benefit from others' experiences. Having researched this topic in-depth will better prepare America's military professionals for future endeavors in areas around the world labeled by Thomas Barnett as —the gap" where the United States military will most likely find itself deployed as either a stability or counterinsurgent force.[1] It is important . . . that the lessons of the past should not be forgotten or ignored, but should be applied to the future.[2]

Colonel Virgil Ney, the Chief of Military History at the Fort Belvoir based Combat Research Group in the early 1960s, stated that philosopher George Santayana —unknowingly made a valuable contribution to the military art" when Santayana declared that —those who do not learn from history will be forced to repeat it."[3] If one subscribes to this belief and sees the value of studying past conflicts, then where does he cast the net in such a broad historical fishing expedition? One avenue of approach would be to look at not only America's recent history, but that of its closest ally who shares a similar culture, similar force structure and comparable national strategy. Since at least the end of World War II, British and American historians and military strategists have collaborated over the lessons learned and principles involved with counterinsurgency efforts in which both countries have participated. From 2001 until the present both countries find

2

themselves fighting, alongside each other once again, in two counterinsurgencies in which the lead commander states that they, at least initially, were lacking the doctrinal answer on to how to fight. This dilemma begs the question of whether or not there are insights from previous counterinsurgencies that American theorists can and should apply to their current conflict. Counterinsurgency is not just thinking man's warfare--it is the graduate level of war.[4]

The initial questions proposed in this work on counterinsurgency are focused on the practitioner level of the counterinsurgency fight. Using an analogy akin to the Special Forces officer's comment, looking at the fight from the tactical and operational levels was possibly defining the undergraduate level analyses of counterinsurgency warfare. In the spirit of Carl von Clausewitz's assertion that military theorists have had to taste the combat that they are writing about or their pontifications will be "impractical or even ridiculous," this manuscript is meant for the practicing counterinsurgent.[5] For they have experienced firsthand not only the friction, but also the incredibly fragile nature of counterinsurgent warfare. Advisors in Iraq and Afghanistan must maintain security for the local populace, while simultaneously training and fighting alongside indigenous forces to kill or capture those extremists that are unwilling to compromise. They must also be ever vigilant not to create more insurgents by targeting innocent civilians.

Another area of interest in writing this thesis, rooted primarily in recent experiences in Iraq, was to look at the methods used in building a host national security apparatus to successfully neutralize the insurgents without creating a breeding ground for future recruitment of follow-on forces for the enemy insurgency. The human element is much more critical to success than either previous Secretaries of Defense Robert

3

McNamara or Donald Rumsfeld's false hope in technology to fight a counterinsurgency. Without the right people doing the job, United States forces can never train, motivate and advise host national security forces to stand up and fight for their country. Since American advisors in Greece did not advise below the corps level, the research did not yield much information on the personalities of the advisors and the results of their efforts. Oman, on the other hand, showed that the British high command, possibly unintentionally, had the right men in the right positions within the Sultan's Armed Forces.

Based on these insights and an understanding of the new counterinsurgency field manual, the initial questions were focused on whether or not the basic doctrinal approach outlined in FM 3-24, *Counterinsurgency* was valid in these previous conflicts. More specifically, this study asks: when comparing the current Army and Marine Corps counterinsurgency doctrine to Oman and Greece, do the experiences in those wars validate or refute the principles and paradoxes for successful counterinsurgency operations as explained in current doctrine?

When studying military doctrine used in the past, a common historical attribute associated to those armies is that they were usually preparing to fight in a manner that they understood to be critical or decisive during the last war. This usually causes a severe learning curve to those armies immediately upon the first bullets being fired. Until they begin to adapt to the new technologies, tactics and the mindset of their enemy, unlike in any other human endeavor, men die. While the military leaders attempt to gain an equal footing with whatever advantage their enemy might have, their casualties mount and their country's will to fight dwindles. In some cases, such as the Battle of Agincourt where the long dominant French heavy cavalry and men-at-arms suffered incredible

casualties at the hands of the English archers, the results both tactically and strategically

are devastating and decisive.[6] Therefore, a constant and incredibly difficult task exists

for military leaders. They must consider how to adapt their doctrine along with new

technologies to not only mitigate their perceived and actual enemy's advantages, but also

to develop improvements that will give their armed forces an edge. As in most cases,

despite previous examples in American history of fighting similar small insurgent wars,

warfighters in the current fight have adapted on the fly.

Despite the current mantra fervently displayed in recruiting videos that the Army

is preparing for the next war that it faces, the question arises: does United States Army

counterinsurgency doctrine have a life span beyond the current battlefield? It is

impossible to look into the future, but one can judge patterns and similarities by

examining the past. More specifically, one can judge the current counterinsurgency

doctrine to see if the fundamentals it espouses were used in previous modern

counterinsurgencies and if they were successful. Conversely, one can see if those same

methods and principles were followed and did they make a significant, decisive

difference in the counterinsurgency effort?

The word –effort" was carefully chosen and replaced the word –fight" because,

although significant military lethal operations are needed in counterinsurgency, the more

decisive and important factors involve standing up and legitimizing the host nation

government to supply its people with basic human needs. Without providing the most

basic of such needs, no government will ever be viewed as legitimate in the eyes of its populace, and the narrative the insurgents are propagating will not only ring true, but in the end will bring down the very government that the United States is trying to support.

In order to analyze what type of battle the United States will fight in the future, one has to make several assumptions. First and foremost is that Thomas Barnett is right in that America will continue to fight in the –gap" regions of the world.[7] Barnett explains that these countries are the third world countries that live on the fringe of the global community and for one reason or another do not take part. Understanding the composition of those regions leads to the next and perhaps easier assumption that the fringe countries in the –gap" will not be able to mount an effective conventional force against a preeminent military machine. With that understood, one must expect that they will choose to fight unconventionally against American forces. A less radical assumption is that American conventional forces will easily defeat whatever conventional force is present and gain control of the ground, but that out of the ashes an insurgency will arise. This is especially true if the Americans are viewed as occupiers and not liberators or if the government that is established is not viewed as legitimate.

Depending on whether or not American forces are treated as liberators or occupiers, the disenfranchised will either join the political process and attempt to make positive change or attempt to depose whatever the established government is by an insurgency. They will most likely label their actions as a revolutionary struggle. In fact, labeling such struggles as insurgencies causes a level of insulation from their root cause which prevents American theorists from identifying the center of gravity in such an effort--ideological motivation. The disenfranchised peoples will have no other military option but to fight unconventionally against America's armed forces.

By looking at the counterinsurgencies of Oman and Greece and comparing those to the Army's current model, one can at least surmise that the truths the United States holds evident for the current fight were also relevant for past conflicts. Another expectation is that one might also be able to weight the recommendations in FM 3-24 based on a comparison to previous fights. If one strategy or aspect seemed important in all the conflicts studied and others less so, then one might conclude it is more relevant than the rest.

Several dangers arise from this approach. One immediate concern is that if one truly wanted to evaluate this doctrine completely, more studies of insurgency conflicts would give the argument more validity. Although the immediate logic of researching and writing an expanded analysis of insurgent forces exists, a more selective study might offer a better analysis. By focusing efforts on two insurgencies involving Western forces, different social, cultural and technological differences that one might note when comparing, for example, Eastern armies will not confuse or skew the results of the study. Although Westerners can clearly learn from studying an Eastern approach to counterinsurgency, the lessons learned from Anglo-American counterinsurgency efforts will more likely correlate to America's current doctrine. From this study one can either confirm the current counterinsurgency doctrine or recommend changes that are likely to fit into American societal cultural norms and be adaptable to American military techniques, tactics and procedures.

Another possible danger that arises in this kind of study is what might work well in one area of the world might not be as effective in others. Each country or region of the world has different topography, climates, cultures, religion and social constructs. Being cognizant of such a danger, this study has endeavored to include those factors in the study of the two different conflicts. Despite some of these differences, there were still qualitative results from the study that lent to an understanding of counterinsurgency operations and primarily supported America's current doctrine.

In order to research the validity of America's counterinsurgency doctrine, this study focused on counterinsurgencies that had some specific similarities. It centered on two relatively modern, limited, yet successful, Anglo-American counterinsurgencies. Two counterinsurgencies that fit that description are the British counterinsurgency operations in Oman and the American counterinsurgency assistance given to Greece. These counterinsurgencies were supported economically and through advisors from outside powerful nations. In neither case did the supporting country provide troop formations in large quantities and in both cases those soldiers sent filled either advisory or leadership roles. Interestingly, despite their success, the Oman and Greece counterinsurgencies are relatively unknown gems of experience from which the professional soldier can glean to gain new perspective on counterinsurgency operations.

Although the impetuses for the rebels fighting these insurgencies differed, several common themes prevailed. Oman and Greece had citizens that were disaffected with their government and those dissidents had internal and external support for the insurgency. Due to multiple factors in both situations, Britain in Oman and the United States in Greece decided to provide limited support to the host government. For this reason, the two efforts relied mostly on indigenous forces to conduct operations against the insurgent forces and both counterinsurgent forces ended up fighting against guerillas.

The second chapter of this study is devoted to the Greek Civil War which took place during the bloodiest decade of the country's existence. On one side stood the Greek national government, with an extensive history of failure and extreme politics, supported by initially Britain and eventually the United States. On the other side stood an insurgent force initiated and led by guerillas and supported by countries but made up of a disparate group of leftists opposed to Greece's Royalist government.

Given limited coverage in John Chamber's volume on American military history, Greece's importance is discussed in the work only in that it was the impetus behind the Truman Doctrine.[8] In fact, the Truman administration's attempts to garner support for Greece eventually would be coined the Truman Doctrine. Although the United States only played a late but decisive part in the war, the ground work for the civil war started as early as the defeat by Turkish forces in 1922 and grew in strength in the 1930s when the Communist Party was driven underground by the then dictator Ioannis Metaxas. Understanding the Axis occupation of Greece provides the context in which the disparate guerilla elements formed against the Axis Armies during the war, and more importantly, how those elements worked against each other to ensure they were in position to assume power at the end of the war.

This paper covers little of the actual civil war in which the United States sent advisors to help the Greek government fight off the guerillas yet this study is about the two successful counterinsurgencies. There are two reasons for this. First, a major contention of this study is that military forces and their operations against an insurgency are only enabling factors. They are critical to provide security or stability and show legitimacy of the government in power, but alone will never defeat an insurgency. The

9

idea of the pen being mightier than the sword or the tongue being mightier than the blade fits within the framework of counterinsurgency and should be of primary focus in American counterinsurgency doctrine. One must attack not the men in an insurgency but the reason or reasons they are fighting. In order to do that, one must understand the operational environment in which they are fighting. That environment not only includes what is happening at the time of the insurgency, but the often overlooked study of the history, culture and central figures of the warring factions.

The third chapter focuses on the British counterinsurgency fight in the Dhofar region of Oman from approximately 1967 to 1975 when the Sultan officially declared victory against the guerillas. This chapter, although still supporting the overall thesis of government legitimacy, also gives valuable insight on the type of men needed to advise and assist operations against an insurgency. With four hundred British officers and non-commissioned officers serving in the Sultan's Armed Forces or embedded in indigenous forces with the British SAS, Oman was clearly not a focus of Britain's world strategy. However, this force structure proved exactly what Sultan Qaboos of Oman needed.

Chapter 4 dissects parts of American counterinsurgency doctrine as outlined in FM 3-24 and compares those beliefs and understanding to the two successful counterinsurgencies of this study. The principles and paradoxes that applied to Greece and Oman are described in how they specifically effected the counterinsurgency fight. Many of these ideas are intertwined and therefore the paradoxes listed in FM 3-24 will be discussed in the larger context of the principle that they support or are linked. American Soldiers and Marines, who are more globally minded than their predecessors of the Philippines War or even the more recent Greece or Oman insurgencies, if told the context of why they are there, will be able to take the general principles from their doctrine and work effectively to support the appropriate end state.

A short conclusion will reiterate the overall purpose direction and final conclusion that this study puts forward. The principles, with the exception of intelligence driven operations, are evaluated. Although intelligence to drive operations is understandably important in counterinsurgency operations, research in Oman and Greece did not provide any insight on this principle. Additionally, the paradoxes of counterinsurgency operations are evaluated in concert with the principles in which they are inherently tied.

> It is necessary to consider the problems facing a government in its approach to its own people at the outset of an open insurgency.[9]

> Organization . . . should be the vital first step in the governing power's strategy to thwart revolutionary attempts . . . It is not so much the form of the administration that counts as the fact that it must be . . . responsive to the needs of the people and readily apparent to them.[10]

Advisors to the Iraqi and Afghani forces have seen firsthand the incredible complexities that fighting a counterinsurgency brings. They understand the importance of the host national military and police forces and their role in the counterinsurgency fight. Despite the difficulties that arise with working with such indigenous forces, with an unfamiliar culture and diverse history from that of their American upbringings, the advisors come away with a unique perspective that such indigenous forces, not the highly trained and well-equipped United States forces, were the decisive element in fighting the counterinsurgent. These advisors realized, incidentally what FM 3-24 states, that the local soldiers know the terrain and the people living there exponentially better than American forces ever will and are therefore in a better position to find, capture or kill the enemy. However, fighting an insurgency at the tactical level runs the danger of losing perspective of the larger fundamentally important aspects of the war. Wrapped up in the details of conducting combat missions and training their counterparts, a danger exists that they might not take the time to see the forest through the trees. The U.S. Army teaches as part of its doctrine the vital importance of ensuring that its subordinates understand the desired end state. The end state in the case of a counterinsurgency is a stable environment in which the local population is thriving, allowing for the foreign counterinsurgency forces to go home. The only way to finally ensure that condition is to ensure that the government is perceived as legitimate not by the advising nation, but by the local population. All military endeavors in such a combat zone must be focused in support of that end state--local, legitimate civilian leadership while the military is an enabler to that success and not the end state itself.

---

[1]Thomas P.M. Barnett, The Pentagon's New Map: War and Peace in the Twenty-First Century (New York: G. P. Putnam's Sons, 2004), 4.

[2]Julian Paget, Counter-Insurgency Operations: Techniques of Guerilla Warfare (New York: Walker and Company, 1967), 155.

[3]Ibid., 7.

[4]Department of the Army, Field Manual (FM) 3-24, Counterinsurgency (Washington, DC: Government Printing Office, 2006), 1-1.

[5]Carl von Clausewitz, On War, trans. Michael Howard and Peter Paret, 13th ed. (New York: Alfred A. Knopf, 1993), 139.

[6]John Keegan, The Face of Battle (London: Penguin Books, 1976), 86-107.

[7]Barnett, The Pentagon's New Map, 7-8.

[8]Howard Jones, "Truman Doctrine," in The Oxford Companion to American Military History, ed. John Whiteclay Chambers II (Oxford: Oxford University Press, 1999), 736-737.

[9]Sir Robert Thompson, Defeating Communist Insurgency: The Lessons of Malaya and Vietnam, Studies in International Security (New York: Praeger, 1966), 63.

[10]John J. McCuen, The Art of Counter-Revolutionary War: The Strategy of Counter-Insurgency (Harrisburg: Stackpole Books, 1966), 85.

CHAPTER 2

GREECE

In many ways Greece provided an ideal setting for Communist insurgent warfare, the people having warlike traditions and a record of resistance to the Turkish regime that was imposed upon them for nearly five hundred years. The very nature of the country and its economy lent themselves to resistance tactics, whether they were conducted against the Axis Occupation Forces, those of the Greek Royal Government, or against the other non-Communist insurgent bands.[1]

-- Edgar O'Ballance, 1966

On an uncharacteristically cold and wet late November day in 1922, six men were placed in line on a barren hilltop field next to the Goudi Military Barracks just outside of Athens. They were the senior Greek leadership responsible for prosecuting a failed war against the Turkish revolutionary forces of the former Ottoman Empire--Greece's 500

14

year oppressor. Starting at the very top, the Prime Minister himself, Georgios Hatzianestis, down through the War, Finance, State and Interior ministers as well as the Commander in Chief of the Greek Army had been tried and found guilty of high treason against the fledgling nation. The war against the former Ottoman Empire had gone so poorly and so many men had died in the failed attack against Constantinople's forces that someone had to pay. The Greek military, in order to maintain its position of protector of the state, had to blame the war on those at the highest level. Greek military tradition, similar to that of the Turkish military, took on the role of protecting the state not only from external enemies, but also internal ones as well, whether they be dissidents or political figures gone awry. In fact, even twenty years after Greece's civil war ended in 1949, army officers felt political intervention was proper if there is an imminent internal Communist takeover, a breakdown in political order and governmental efficiency, [or] a pervasive social decay in morals and public standards."[2] Unlike previous coups, however, this time blood had to be spilled.

The Greek people demanded someone pay for the massive failure at the Battle of Dumlupinar in August of 1922 in which the Turkish Army routed the numerically superior Greek Army. One soldier who had been wounded on the front lines fighting the Turkish Army demanded to be part of the firing squad. The commander of the firing squad fought with another bystander who looked like he might have been planning to snap a photograph. After realizing the man did not have a camera, the firing squad commander returned to his heavy task of executing the senior leadership of his country. There were five men designated as the firing squad for each guilty party except the Chief of Staff who had six due to the demands of the wounded soldier. On command, the firing

15

squad shot and five of the six immediately collapsed. The former field marshall of the Greek Army clutched his throat and spun downward to the earth. The wounded soldier shot another round into the senior military man and the explosion of his cranium marked the beginning of a bloody two decades.[3]

This bloody coup marked the end of the —Great Idea" in which Greek politicians called for a return to the expanded territory and people that Ancient Greece controlled during its apex of power. It also marked the beginning of a twenty year period of instability and signified the very essence of Greek government and its people.[4] The Ottoman rulers tolerated some local Greek governance, but did not develop an in-depth educational system nor did they grow any form of an effective government structure within the Greek community that could run a stable and legitimate government once Greece gained its independence.[5] When Britain first helped Greece gain its independence from the Ottoman Empire in 1829, the country imported royalty from Germany to run its country. It attempted other forms of governance including democracy. However, despite being the birthplace of democracy, Greece's later attempt at this most representative form of governance came at a time when the realities of Greece's weak economy during a world depression gave the perception of a flawed system and the government was quickly replaced through another coup.[6]

Although an example of a successful counterinsurgency, Greece is overlooked and almost unknown outside military history channels. Its importance as the only European country after World War II to successfully defeat a Communist insurgency is all but forgotten outside of Greece.[7] By the end of German occupation during World War II Greece was ripe for an insurgency. In fact, its history was full of conflict with larger powers that led Greek men and woman to adopt a guerilla strategy to fight the more powerful invaders. Unable to deter their invaders from occupation, Greeks had three choices. They either joined a guerilla force determined on fighting the occupying forces, got along as best as possible, or actively supported the invaders. To the Greek defenders during the German occupation, however, there were only two choices. They either fought against them or joined them. There was no middle ground, for attempting to get along was the same as collaboration. This in turn split the Greek people into the two opposing contingents, setting the stage for their decade long civil war.[8]

Despite centuries of being ruled by either the Roman or Ottoman Empires, the Greek people have maintained a sense of ―Greekness" centered on their families which gave them a feeling of individuality far more powerful than the nationalistic sentiment of being part of a state. Until the second half of the 20th century, in the face of occupation by those powers, the mountains and the seas had separated the majority of the Greeks from the urban centers along the coast. This separation allowed Greeks living in the mountains separate, unique, and independent identity to flourish.[9] As connections between these urban centers started reaching these independent subsistence farming villages, conflict occurred in the form of a civil war. A clash of cultures and competing ideals ensued.

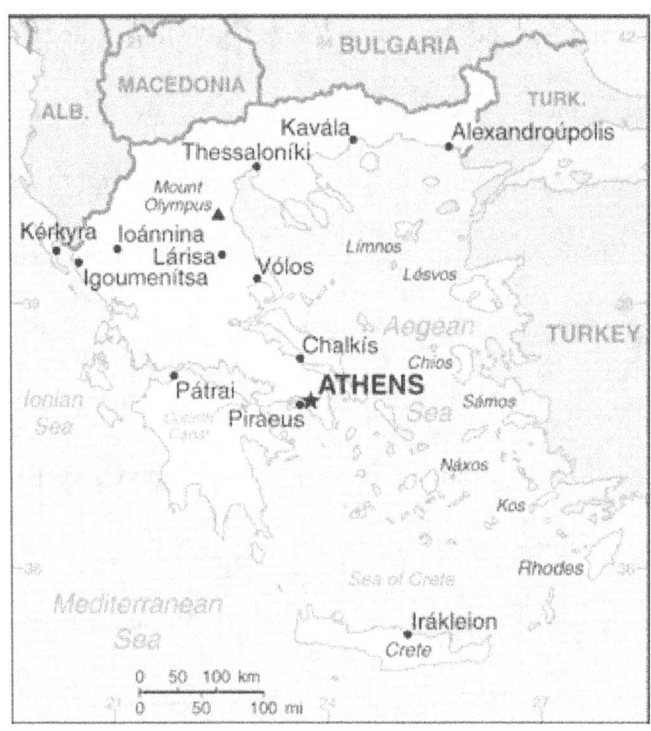

Figure 2. CIA World Book
Source: CIA World Book, Map of Greece, www.cia.gov (accessed 11 March 2009).

Made up of over 2,000 islands, of which approximately 170 are inhabited, 15,000

kilometers of coastline and large formations of mountainous terrain that covers three

quarters of the nation's surface, Greece sits on the southern side of the European

continent and the northern side of the Mediterranean. Its land mass, 131,957 square

kilometers, is slightly smaller than the state of Alabama and due to the differences in

terrain and the separation of the mountains, especially the Pindus, the country is divided

up into nine distinctly different, regional areas. It has three rivers, the Vardar, Struma

and Nestos, that provide ―irregular seasonal levels that make them unreliable for

navigation and irrigation," and drain into deep gorges to the north and northwest of

Greece into present day states of Albania and Macedonia.[10] About half of the population lived in the plains in mainland Greece or the coastal regions of the Peloponnese. Athens and Piraeus were the two largest cities with populations of 400,000 and 300,000, respectively, but only another twenty or so cities had populations exceeding 20,000 people. About ten percent of Greeks live on one of the 170 inhabited islands and the other forty percent live in small mountain villages that encompass the area where much of the brutal fighting during the German occupation and subsequent civil war took place.[11]

Greece's strategic location brought the country to the forefront of European importance around the turn of the 20th century. Indeed like Turkey, Greece controls critical sea routes to Istanbul, the Bosporus and the Black Sea. Similar to Oman and the critical Strait of Hormuz, such strategic locations made Greece important to the world's western powers. In fact, its location near Turkey made it important even before Greece's declaration of independence from the Ottoman Empire. What turned out to be a significant factor in foreign powers determining Greece's strategic importance was the country's overland transportation routes from central Europe to the Mediterranean ports. Thus in the 1940s, during the ―most devastating and deadly" decade in Greece's 3,000 year history, Hitler used Greece as an embarkation point to resupply Erwin Rommel's Afrika Corps.[12] But unlike the times of Alexander the Great, the Byzantine Empire or the powerful Spartan armies, Greece no longer had the capacity to conquer other nations or even effectively defend its borders from a first rate military.

The Hellenic Army can trace its lineage back almost 190 years, after winning its independence from Turkey in 1829. The Ottoman Empire did not officially accept Greek independence, however, until it signed the Treaty of Constantinople in 1832. The

19

modern Greek military did not thrive because it did not have an industrial base. This deficiency was obvious at the Battle of Dumlupinar, in August 1922, against Mustafa Kemal Ataturk, the Turkish revolutionary general and future first president of the newly formed Turkish state. Although Greek forces held strong defensive positions and had numerical superiority over Ataturk's forces, Turkish heavy artillery played a decisive role in weakening Greek positions. Just prior to the hostilities in 1940, the dictator General Ioannis Metaxas significantly improved the Greek military as a precaution to an ever growing Italian threat. Metaxas' preparations proved effective against the Italian forces but were no match for Germany's modern army.

Greece in the 20th century was an incredibly poor country made even poorer during World War II as the German Army wicked away its wealth in manpower, agriculture and natural resources. A weak national government failed either through incompetence or corruption to right any of these wrongs. An example of this mismanagement can be seen clearly in agriculture. Despite Greece producing insufficient food to support its population, luxury food products such as grapes, olives, dried fruit, and wines were grown primarily for export.[13] Despite these shortcomings many Greek citizens longed for a return to the Greek empire and better days.

After Greece gained its independence in 1829, it attempted to regain a lost identity. Lacking a ruling family of its own, Greece imported King Otho of Bavaria but he became much more autocratic then the Greeks had expected. After Otho was overthrown in 1843, they sought their own national identity based on that of better Greek times.[14]

Constantinople was to be the new Greek nation's capitol. This —Great Idea"

formed in 1844, not only gave reasons for Greece's poor standing, but also laid the

foundation of its national strategy for almost the next century.

> The Greek kingdom is not the whole of Greece, but only a part, the
> smallest poorest part. A native is not only someone who lives within this
> kingdom, but also one who lives in Ioannia, in Thessaly, in Serres, in Adrianople,
> in Constantinople, in Trebizond, in Crete, in Samos and in any land associated
> with Greek history or the Greek race.

> --Ioannis Kolettis, 1844[15]

In order to accomplish this expansion, a succession of different forms of

government led by various monarchs and ministers had taken place. Poverty and failed

government reforms led to rebellions and coups. A new leader, government, or plan

would take power, and after being unable to change Greece's plight, the government

would either give way to a new or previous government. This pattern continued until the

beginning of the 20th century.

Unable to solve its internal misfortunes, Greek leaders turned outward to improve

their standing. Greece, however, was unable to tackle Turkey on its own and so looked

for allies to gain back some of its glory and reestablish the old kingdom. Prior to 1912,

Greece joined Bulgaria, Serbia, Montenegro, and Albania in what would be known as a

Balkan Pact of Christian Nations to attack a waning Ottoman Empire and take back lands

that once belonged to Christian Europe.[16] This fit in perfectly with Greece's move

toward its Great Idea and despite rifts in the alliance originating from division of land in

the Treaty of Bucharest in August of 1913, Greece came out very favorably. Greece

increased its land mass by seventy percent by pushing Ottoman Army as far back as the

port city of Thessaloniki. This large increase also swelled Greece's population from

21

2,800,000 to 4,800,000.[17] This would be the impetus behind a schism that pushed Greece to almost virtual collapse. Far from being Greek, many new inhabitants were foreign. Sephardic Jews, Slavs, large numbers of Muslim Turks and Vlachs who spoke anything from Romanian to Spanish now reluctantly became part of Greece. This also had an interesting effect of dampening the spread of Communism. Newly conquered territories of Greece formed guerilla forces to fight German occupation forces from 1941 to 1944 but, due to their distrust of their newly acquired countrymen, they did not welcome the Communist guerillas into their areas.[18] This neutralized much of the support Bulgaria gave to the Communist insurgents during the civil war and the reason they were primarily restricted to the Vitsi and Grammos areas along the Yugoslavian and Albanian borders (refer to map figures 2-3).

During World War I, despite Greece's King Constantine's ties to Germany and his desire to stay neutral, Greece joined the side of the *Entente* and fought against the Central powers.[19] As Germany and the Ottoman Empire lost the war, Greek nationalists saw an opportunity to strive again for their ―Great Idea." Although attacks against the newly formed Republic of Turkey initially went well, skillfully planned and executed counterattacks by Turkish forces routed Greek forces from Asia Minor, ending a 2,500 year Greek presence on the western littoral of Asia Minor. With the horrible rout in Smyrna in the fall of 1922, a million Greeks were displaced into a struggling Greek economy.[20] After Greek military forces overthrew the government and executed the senior leadership, a state of constant unrest besieged the country for next 20 years. King George II, Crown Prince to King Constantine who abdicated the throne in 1922, had sat at the thrown less than a year after succeeding his father. He was asked to leave in

October 1923, after a failed coup, but did not abdicate the throne as his father had.

Between 1924 and 1935 when the king returned there were 23 changes in government,

one dictatorship and thirteen separate coups.[21] This unrest brought with it many forms of

dissidence, such as the socialist movement.

The Greek Communist Party (KKE) grew out of the Greek Socialist Party (SEK)

which, after watching the Bolshevik Revolution gain strength in Russia at the end of

World War I, applied to join the Communist International Movement or Comintern.

Although initially started by intellectuals, inspired by the Bolshevik Revolution in

Russia, the movement heavily recruited tobacco, industrial, and railway workers, many of

which were refugees from the Ottoman Empire.[22] The central committee of the

Comintern accepted the SEK's request for funds and on September 21st 1920 announced

that the Communist Party of Greece had been unanimously accepted. The SEK became

the Greek Communist Party or KKE overnight and hoped the international power of the

Communism would make up for the lack of strength within the Greek Party.[23]

The Greek Communist Party initially adopted a strategy of what it termed –a long

period of lawful existence." Although it quickly denounced the country's war against the

Ottoman Empire, it chose to conduct its activities as a political party. In 1935 Nicholas

Zakhariadis was named the Greek Secretary General to the party.[24] Reacting to the anti-

war propaganda being spread by the party, the Greek government took some measures

against the KKE, but it was not until the mid 1930s, when the KKE had gained a little

momentum, that the party was driven underground.[25] Despite being outlawed, members

of the Communist party were not the only Greeks disaffected by the government at the time. If Greece was to succeed, a more moderate and representative approach was needed.

Understanding this when exiled King George II returned to Greece in 1935, he initially made steps to bring the Venizelist and pro-monarchists closer together. He dismissed General Georgios Kondylis, the Greek prime minister turned regent, who had brought the King back into power, primarily because the general's viewpoints were extreme and Kondylis was unwilling to reconcile. The King also called the two parties together to ask them to set aside their differences to establish a viable government. Partisanship prevailed however and as the parties attempted to gain favor with the KKE, army officers came forward to the King and explained that the army could not remain on the sidelines while collaboration with the Communist Party took place. The anti-war slogans during the previous war had finally caught up with them. In order to prevent an overthrow, the King appointed Ioannis Metaxas, former Greek Chief of Staff and Royalist Party member, as Minister of War and the stage was set for dissolution of the Communist Party as a lawful political entity.[26]

Despite the fact that the Greek Communist Party only gained about nine percent of the vote in 1935, that along with their activities was enough to spur a significant anti-Communist crackdown by then dictator Ioannis Metaxas in 1936. In May, 1936, the rioting that took place in Thessaloniki looked as if the Communists were creating conditions similar to that of the Bolsheviks and the "masses" were being prepared for a general assault on the government. An article written in *Rizospatstis*, the official newspaper of the Greek Communist Party, seemed to confirm a genuine threat from the KKE. The article stated that Greece will not see a peace again "no matter how much of

24

the people's blood may be spilled," until the monarchy was overthrown and the people took control.[27] On 5 August the Communist Party called for a general strike to protest a bill being proposed that imposed mandatory arbitration in labor disputes. Metaxas used this to get King George II to agree to disbanding parliament and mobilizing the Greek industries' work force to maintain essential services. Metaxas also censored the press and eventually outlawed Communism.[28] From 1936 until 1945, the Communist Party was outlawed within Greece and therefore its members were pushed underground and moved from a political party to a revolutionary guerilla force.[29] Their only solution to such oppressive behavior was to overthrow Metaxas via a civil war or a coup.[30] The Communist Party attempted this three times in the next fifteen years: once during the German occupation between 1943-1944; again in December 1944, and finally during a three year civil war from 1946-1949.[31]

Ironically the very threat and ultimate reality of Greece's worst decade, during the 1940s, was the source of inspiration for his new government structure. Sick of politicians and Greek individuality, Metaxas admired Fascist Italian and German societal structure. After failed elections in 1936, Metaxas was appointed the interim prime minister, a position he eventually turned into a dictatorship. He quickly suppressed opposition including the Communist Party and began the creation of the ―Third Hellenic Civilization," (the first was the pagan civilization; the second was the Christian Byzantine Empire; and, the third had Metaxas as its founder). He declared himself the ―first peasant," the ―first worker" and liked being known as the ―national father." Trade between Germany and Greece doubled and although he continued mandatory arbitration he also declared a moratorium on peasant debts. Metaxas also created the National

Youth Organization which promoted Greek nationalism and had compulsory attendance.

He reorganized the Greek military and his decisive actions in government highlighted the

failures of the indecisive parliamentary system.[32] This had the additional effect of

diminishing leadership from other political members, that, had they not been ostracized

under Metaxas, might have been able to rally Greek forces during the Nazi occupation.

Only the Communist Party with its international recognition within the Comintern

seemed to wield any legitimacy to the Greek people.[33] While the Greek dictator

reorganized his government and military, across the Adriatic Sea the Italian Dictator,

Benito Mussolini was reorganizing his for war.

Mussolini had been so expansionist and aggressive that Turkey signed the Balkan

Pact with the same states that attacked it just a decade earlier. This was an attempt to

show a united front against Italian aggression, but the Italian dictator was determined to

carve out his own empire in the Mediterranean. After conquering Albania in 1939, he

attempted to provoke Prime Minister Metaxas and King George to give him a pretext to

invade Greece.[34] Despite his many attempts Greece did not budge. Meanwhile, countries

across Europe were falling into Axis hands. Already Poland, Czechoslovakia, Denmark,

Luxemburg, Norway, Holland, Belgium, and France had fallen. Only England continued

to hold on by winning the Battle of Britain. Mussolini finally grew inpatient by October

1940 and sent the Italian ambassador to Greece, Count Emmanuele Grazzi, to put an

ultimatum on Metaxas at three o'clock in the morning. Thirty minutes prior to the 0530

deadline Mussolini's divisions attacked Greece from Albania.[35] Mussolini's bark was,

however, worse than his bite and Metaxas' army was able to decisively stop the invading

Italians and push them back into Albania.

Although Hitler's initial intentions were to leave Italy to take care of Albania, Greece and Yugoslavia, Italian blundering in Africa and Greece, along with the German Luftwaffe's failure in the Battle of Britain, caused Hitler to focus efforts on Greece. Although Britain had started to loosen its tentacles in Athens, fear of Mussolini's move on Greece's Albanian neighbors drove Britain and France to declare their support for Greece's integrity. In the eyes of many Greek citizens, however, Britain's weak showing in the Munich Pact of 1938 made their earlier overtures for support appear worthless.[36] It must also be remembered that Greece was Britain's last ally on the continent with four British divisions defending it and was one way for Hitler to successfully hurt his otherwise untouchable enemy. In the end, however, Italian soldiers lacked the heart for such an invasion as they had no good reason to invade Greece. The Greeks were fighting for their country and did so tenaciously. The result was that Mussolini's weakened divisions were easily thrown back into Albania and Hitler was forced to commit German divisions to bail out his Italian protégé.[37]

Initial hope by the Greek people at seeing the confident British forces moving to Greece's northern border was quickly replaced by more hopelessness as Germany attacked. Unlike the Italians, the Germans unremittingly drove through Greek and British resistance. The British, Australian and New Zealand troops fought at Thermopylae against the advancing German army as Leonidas had done against the Persians almost 2,500 years earlier. With similar expectations, the defenders knew they were fighting a rear guard action so that British Coalition and Greek troops could withdraw from Athens. As Leonidas' heroic stand worked against Xerxes' army so did this one. Nearly 50,000 troops and King George's government were evacuated from Athens before German

troops entered the city.[38]

Because King George and his government went into exile before German forces

reached Athens, the resistance movement in Greece was disorganized and ad hoc. Many

different guerilla forces quickly established themselves within Greece. The larger

guerilla forces that were more nationalist and employed officers of the Greek Army had

28

several names. Initially known as the National Band of Greek Guerillas (EAO), they quickly changed their name to the National Republic of Greek League or in Greek *Ethnikos Dimokratikos Ellinikos Syndesmos* (EDES). EDES was led by General Napolean Zervas and unlike ELAS (Communist guerillas) Zervas was separate and did not work under the political wing of EDES. Since General Zervas had the military force behind him, his political counterpart in Athens, General Plasteias, became ineffectual with Zervas eventually wielding most of the Royalist power.[39]

Although there were many other disparate guerilla organizations that fought against the occupying German forces and each other, the primary guerilla organization was ELAS. The military wing of the Communist Party EAM or KKE, ELAS was initially very successful in recruiting young Greek men, with the unusual help of Prime Minister Metaxas, who printed a letter written by the then imprisoned Secretary of the KKE, Niko Zachariadis. In this letter, Zachariadis stated ―in this war which is directed by the Metaxas Government, all of us should give our whole strength without reservation."[40] Although later refuted by the Comintern as fake, this letter gave the KKE ―national and patriotic credentials" willing to fight beyond that of the national government which fled the country.[41] Additionally, ELAS had several distinct advantages over the other guerilla forces that made it significantly more capable to recruit men to their bands of guerillas. The governmental collapsed without establishing a resistance network coupled with the fact that many republican and royalist leaders established security battalions to fight against the guerilla forces in the mountains was a significant advantage. Whatever their reasons, royalists and republicans were seen by many Greeks as collaborators. Additionally, Metexas' heavy handed approach and the dissolution of Greece's government pushed many Greek people to an alternative which at least purportedly was for the people. Being driven underground and having direct supervision over the ELAS forces, the KKE was able to get their propaganda about their military organization and therefore able to recruit additional forces out much better than other guerilla forces. Because most of the guerillas were not associated to any political party or in other cases like EDES their political and military branch were not closely associated, those forces were not recruiting or working on a national level. ELAS and KKE were national and therefore had a much greater nationwide draw.[42]

ELAS, although no friend of the Nazi occupiers, was more concerned with consolidating power for what they foresaw as eventual Greek independence. For this reason they worked begrudgingly with British advisors from General Headquarters only because they were worried about Colonel Zervas' EDES getting all the credit and therefore the equipment and training support from the British. An example of this cooperation came in the form of the attack on the Hellada Gorge railway section. In late November 1942, a British sabotage team worked with not only 45 EDES members, but also 115 ELAS members. This joint cooperation was carefully designed within the ELAS so as to show cooperation for a mission that would have been executed with or without their support.[43] For ELAS correctly assumed that if EDES was receiving credit and arms for their exploits in helping the British defeat the German occupying forces then they would also be in better position to recruit men into their ranks and therefore be a bigger threat to ELAS/ELAM plans at the conclusion of the war.

Unlike any of the other guerilla bands, however, thanks to Metaxas' driving the Communist Party underground, ELAS was already prepared for a covert existence. The organization had recruited men, subverted people and was much more capable to organize, recruit and equip their fighters. This, in many Greeks' eyes, looked like the unit to join to attrit, harass and eventually expel the invading German army. Having tens of thousands of guerilla forces and being the largest force by far, ELAS, as early as 1942, started attacking other guerilla bands. Although it was unable to defeat General Zervas' EDES, ELAS was, however, able to destroy many smaller bands of guerilla forces. Typically members of these other bands were either brought into the Communist guerilla force or they were executed. The British attempted to maintain some sort of unity amongst the guerilla forces so that they would focus on fighting the Germans instead of each other. Several times the British provided weapons and money as rewards for signing peace agreements or attacking German or Italian forces.[44]

After the Allies invaded Italy in 1943, the Italian forces that were left in Greece either attempted to withdraw or in the case of one Italian division attempted to join Greece's fight against the German forces. Initially, the Italians and their arms and equipment were brought into the fight, but ELAS worried about a diminishing sense of balance and mistrusting the Italian invaders, called for their disarmament and surrender. Upon the Italian surrender ELAS took the equipment of the entire division and used that equipment and ammunition to renew attacks on other guerilla organizations.[45]

Having had years of failed government and remembering the absolute powers under Metaxas, many guerilla forces, each with their own agendas, sought to consolidate power as the occupying forces withdrew. Despite British efforts, guerilla forces continued to clash. ELAS being the largest guerilla force fared much better than the others. EDES was the only force able to significantly withstand attacks from the bigger

31

guerilla force and between 1943 and 1944 the guerilla forces clashed repeatedly. In February 1944 with help from the British an uneasy cease fire was arranged between EDES and ELAS called the Plaka Agreement. Along with the British promising to supply the fighting organizations across the board more fairly, prisoners were exchanged and an agreement for a cessation of hostilities was agreed upon.[46] Both Churchill and Stalin talked during this time, and against the United States' wishes, the two agreed to split Europe into spheres of influence. They decided that the Soviet Union would have influence over Romania and Bulgaria and Great Britain would maintain influence over Yugoslavia and Greece. Such taciturn agreement between the two along with President Roosevelt's final acquiescence to Churchill's meddling gave the British prime minister free rein in Greece. Despite worries about the new government, the Comintern ordered the KKE to join the government during the Lebanon meeting.[47] The agreement in Lebanon was that all of ELAS would take orders from a common command.[48]

The Greek government of National Unity returned to Greece on October 18, 1944, to a divided country with much less legitimacy then when it had left. Not only had the government squashed any form of representation prior to the war, but it had fled the country leaving the Greek people to fend for themselves against the Nazi army. Prime Minister George Papandreou in his first address called for national unity to save the country. Communists who had been outlawed and forced underground before the occupation were now seen as freedom fighters and national heroes and were not ready to give up those gains. Papandreou over the next month and a half set the stage to take this dangerous and de-stabilizing power away from the Communists by building up volunteer National Guard units and calling for all guerilla forces to turn in their arms by December

10, 1944. ELAS refused to obey and ordered their units toward Athens where many Communist supporters had already occupied sections of the city.[49] The Royalist view was that this was an attempt to seize control of the city while Communists state that they were just demonstrating against Prime Minister Papandreou's political moves. Either way, a bloody brawl ensued.

General Ronald Scobie, the British commander responsible for the British and Greek forces, issued a statement of support for the constitutionally elected government and brought troops, tanks and armored personnel carriers into Athens. Churchill's intent to use force if needed was clear to General Scobie. The British and Greek troops controlled the city center and the Communists controlled the suburbs. On December 3, 1944, with the war still going strong in Europe shots rang out in Constitution square as protestors approached one of the police stations. Each side claimed the other had shot first. Communist hopes that the British would take a hands off approach to the fighting prompted KKE leadership to order protesters to avoid clashes with British troops, however the guerillas collided with British troops as they attempted to take control of the center of the city. Skobie only had a total of 16,000 troops under his command and it was clear that was insufficient to secure a city the size of Athens against a numerically superior 26,000 guerillas.[50]

Despite the fact that the battle did not spread beyond the city and that the fighting lasted for 33 days, the fighting was so fierce that 11,000 people were killed and parts of Athens lay in rubble. Winston Churchill personally went to Athens to solve the dilemma. He pressured King George to accept Archbishop Damaskinos as his regent in Greece and Prime Minister Papandreou was replaced with the more liberal General Nicolas Plastiras.

In Varkiza, near Athens, ELAS and the Greek Minister of Foreign Affairs came to an agreement for a tentative peace; in return for Plastiras being emplaced as a regent until elections could be held. ELAS would turn over their weapons. ELAS members were granted amnesty, all citizens were granted free speech and there was to be a plebiscite on the constitution of Greece.[51]

ELAS instead gave up only about 40,000 largely unserviceable weapons, caching the better weapons for future fighting. Additionally around four thousand of the hard core ELAS members chose instead of returning to their homes to seek safe havens across the border in neighboring states.[52] Despite ELAS grievances and the failure to follow the Varkiza Agreement exactly, Greek government violations of the agreement were even worse. In what was to be known as the period of ―White Terror,‖ from 1945 to 1946, the Ministry of Justice along with vigilante bands of anti-Communists, ignored the amnesty given and began to round up guerilla fighters and prosecute and execute those that were known to kill collaborators. Tax collectors under the PEEA Government (*Politiki Epitropi Ethikis Apeleftherosis),* an autonomous government established by Communists as a reaction to the Nazi collaborationist government, were jailed for the collection of illegal taxes. Many ELAS guerilla heroes became war criminals. In fact, anyone known to have any leftist connections was in danger of these brigands. The KKE had little choice but to either leave the country or go into hiding.[53]

Although the Communist Party's Secretary General at the time of the Varkiza Agreement was Nikos Zahariadis, an unswerving Communist who fully embraced the Comintern, while he was imprisoned by the Germans in France the party was run by George Siantos. Siantos, a veteran trade unionist who grew up as a poor tobacco worker in central Greece, was more concerned with class struggle then Communist doctrine and he was also fearful of Britain's power and long standing dominant role within Greece.[54] So it was Siantos, not Zahariadis, who sought peace with the new Greek government.[55]

Zahariadis was freed from German internment by allied forces and returned to Greece in May of 1945 after the period of White Terror had already commenced. He immediately resumed control and redirected the Greek Communist Party not on a path of political action but of Communist revolution. After Siantos' mysterious death, in 1947 Zahariadis denounced him as a traitor and a British agent.[56] To many Communist Party outsiders it appeared that the Communist Party purposely lied in its concurrence to the Varkiza Agreements. They argued that the Communists made this agreement planning all the time to violate the accord when they were prepared for open armed conflict for overthrow of the Greek government.[57]

Although Greek Communists would argue the agreement was broken upon the

outbreak of the ―White Terror campaigns," Royalists argue that the agreement was broken on the night of March 30, 1946, when Communist guerillas attacked a small village in Thessaly, killing all the local gendarmes and burning several houses to the ground. This attack was quickly followed by numerous other Communist attacks across Greece. Instructions were also sent out to abstain from voting in the elections the following day. Of the 317 seats available, KKE only seated seventeen representatives while the pro-Royalist party seated 191 candidates.[58] The method and results of the election marked a clear turning point for KKE to move from a political to a military solution.

ELAS knew that it was not strong enough to win a decisive battle against the Greek Government forces. The Greek Communist Party estimated it needed an army of 50,000 which was the greatest estimate of guerilla fighters that ELAS claimed during World War II. At its height in 1948 the Communist Democratic Army only was able to boast around 25,000 poorly armed troops.[59] Because of this limiting factor, the guerillas instead chose to wage a war of attrition. In late 1945 and early 1946 they focused on quick, nighttime raids on weakly defended villages. By mid-December the Communist forces controlled about four-fifths of the Greek countryside and British led Greek National Guard units controlled only the center of Athens.[60] These attacks garnered more recruits, kept the government forces on the defensive, and delegitimized the new government for its inability to protect its people.[61] In order to accomplish this task ELAS needed to organize its forces appropriately.

Guerilla forces within ELAS can be broken down into the three distinct groups: the actual fighters, the collaborators and the reserve forces waiting in Albania, Yugoslavia and Bulgaria. The first group's numbers varied from as little as 2,500 men in

37

1946 to as high as 26,000 sometime in 1948. Motivation to join rebel groups varied from everything from economic deprivation amongst the mountain people to a fear of government backlash against anyone suspected of ties with the Communists or leftist leanings. Proof of government backlash being a motivating factor is confirmed by a positive correlation of increased recruitment in the Democratic Army and the Ministry of Justice's mass arrests and deportations without any trials in March of 1947. Although there is speculation of forced recruitment taking place in remote villages other cases of veteran fighters pressuring young Greek men to join, is also very likely. Other than some examples of both being reported there has never been a study that shows the percentage of methods used by the guerilla forces to recruit young men and women into their folds. The collaborators did not fight, but provided intelligence, security, administrative work and logistical support for the Communist fighters.[62]

Although the guerilla forces had artillery and a cavalry brigade, they were never able to employ either during any of their battles so their effects as combat multipliers were negligible. ELAS also had a cavalry brigade. As their ranks increased in 1947 guerilla elements moved from to company and battalion sized formations and in 1948 at the height of guerilla fighting strength they formed some battalions into brigades of 600-800 men. Eventually at Nikos Zakhariadis' direction ELAS gave directions to build up a large conventional army.[63] In May 1948, there were eight divisions broken down into 42 infantry battalions with 43 separate companies. Despite having division formations the guerilla component was never a combined army.[64] It lacked any coordination or effective use of artillery, tanks or airplanes. All this reorganization truly meant, was larger formations of infantry.

The nature of the war initially favored the guerillas. Although significantly outnumbered and outgunned, they maintained the initiative by attacking Greek Army's supply lines, friendly cities, and small outposts at will. Steep slopes, and poor, limited roads inhibited the Greek Army's movements. Slow moving government forces were unable to effectively pursue the Communist guerillas, and therefore resorted to clearing an area, then holding it, which caused the guerillas to go into defensive positions. When government forces did conduct their slow moving offensive operations, the guerillas could hide in the caves and forests.[65]

The Greek Government countered these guerilla forces with armor, artillery, engineers and armored reconnaissance units, but primarily infantry forces. The National Defense Corps which was mostly older reservists, conducted static defenses in the towns and villages. These amounted to little more than lucrative targets for the Communist guerilla forces conducting nightly raids. The Gendarmerie did not fare much better and although these forces were initially used to attack the Communist guerillas, their lackluster performance caused them to fall to a secondary role of supporting the Greek army. The Greek military did raise an effective branch of commando units that were used to chase down the guerillas using tactics similar to that of the enemy. They were mobile, heavily armed, and had significant esprit de corps from their elite status and battlefield victories. The total strength of the government ground forces during the war was estimated at 150,000 Greek national army soldiers, 50,000 National Defense Corps soldiers, 25,000 Gendarmerie, and 7,500 civil police.[66]

British and U.S. viewpoints differed on how to stop the war. Britain, embroiled in in Greece throughout World War II, had immediately started conducting stability

39

operations upon the German withdrawal. Churchill and Great Britain saw Greece as a fight to stop Communist expansion. Despite his earlier arrangement with Stalin, Churchill still was convinced that if the Communists were not stopped in Greece they could spread to Italy. In reality, Stalin true to his word gave little if no support to the Communist movement in Greece.[67] Roosevelt and the United States, from their detached point of view, saw King George's stance as uncompromising, and as a backlash from those who did not want a return of a dictator.[68]

American analysis of Greece's problems stemmed from the Greek political leaders. Their inability to establish a stable and efficient government in Greece . . . greatly retarded economic, social and political rehabilitation," following the war.[69] This failure left the door open to the Greek Communist Party (KKE) to further delegitimize the government and create internal disorder with the eventual goal of taking over Greece. The Greek government, luckily, had an ally in President Harry Truman. Truman, in defending his stance on Greece, stated, that the world had to realize that America's policy was to defend freedom wherever it was threatened."[70] On March 12, 1947, President Truman went before Congress recommending military and economic assistance. In what would be the impetus behind the Truman Doctrine, the President stated it must be the policy of the United States to support the free peoples who are resisting subjugation by armed minorities or by outside pressure."[71] Truman asked Congress for $400 million for both Greece and Turkey and for approval to send both civilian and military advisors.[72]

There was some significant opposition. Fear of extending the Monroe Doctrine to the entire world was a legitimate concern. Anxiety about the United States quickly becoming involved in another war was also a reason for dissension within the congressional ranks. Lastly, some critics argued that conflicts so far away from American borders were the responsibility of the United Nations. The opposition, however, was disjointed and came from both left and right and the messages were so disparate that they failed to rally much support. American newspapers backed the president to the fullest. *Time* magazine stated that if the United States did not act the ―Iron Curtain would be moved down to the Mediterranean." *Newsweek* reported that if America did not act on Greece, there would be a ―disastrous chain reaction affecting America's strategic interests all over the world."[73]

The United Nations Security Commission of Investigation and the Porter economic mission, established by the Truman Administration, declared that Greece had deteriorated so badly that ―only military assistance could achieve the security necessary [for] economic security."[74] For this reason the aid would be split into two accounts, but the majority of the money would go to economic aid. Congress had authorized $300 million in aid with another $50 million already designated for Greece from the United Nations Relief and Rehabilitation Administration (UNRRA). Additionally, Congress authorized the Reconstruction Finance Corporation to make Greece a $100 million advance to Greece that would be paid back once Congressional appropriations for the bill went into effect. Half of the $300 million was designated for war material to support the Greek National Army in its fight against the guerillas. The remainder of the money was to be spent by civilian advisors on relief, rehabilitation and reconstruction. This money was to be a grant as opposed to a loan because the Greek situation was so dire, but there was serious doubts to whether the government would be able to pay it back.[75]

The United States brought a huge bureaucracy to accomplish this mission. Initially, over 800 people alone would be utilized in the communications center in Athens. The headquarters, located next to but separate from the embassy, would be staffed with eight civilian subdivisions. It is important to note that despite the dire military situation, the Department of the Army was initially only to provide about forty military advisors to the Greek National Army. The focus was an economic and political one, using all the branches of government. The State Department urged all departments within the United States government to take part. The Departments of Treasury, Agriculture, Commerce, Labor, Social Security Administration, Public Roads Administration, Federal Security Agency, Bureau of Budget, Corps of Engineers as well as the War and the Navy Departments would take part in the mission.[76]

Although the War Department had already started sending surplus planes to the Greek Government in April 1947, the Greek-Turkish aid bill overwhelmingly passed with bipartisan support in both the House and Senate and became law on May 22, 1947.[77] The bill stated that the American mission's objective was to maintain the ―international security and the national integrity and survival of Greece as a free self-respecting democracy and thereby to contribute to the security and independence of all freedom, loving people."[78] America did not attempt to make any suggestions for exclusion of any political groups, but based on the public reasoning for its support, Washington pushed for a broad, moderate cabinet that excluded fanatical parties on both the left and right. This exclusion applied to the Communists and their sympathizers on the left and ―reactionary rightists" on the extreme right.[79]

The United States, since becoming a world superpower, had fared far better than any other country in World War II, and was willing to help Greece's struggling economy and diminishing security situation. The motivation behind its help may not have been altruistic, but the final result ended up having the winning formula for success. As a result of the incredible increases in production during the war, the United States required about three times the raw materials that it did prior to the war. Greece played an important role in ensuring those resources. James Forrestal, then, Secretary of Defense who had been crucial for mobilizing the industrial war effort stated that the ―survival of our economy" through the procurement of ―materials in those countries . . . is the only thing that makes any impression on me."[80] His business associate stated that if political or social factors were the only factors for intervention in Greece, then ―the hell with it."[81] Louis Halle, a State Department official, stated, ―It was not possible to tell the American people what the real issue was." Luckily, for the benefit of Greece the public relations people within the Truman administration won out. Promotion of democratic principles became the public impetus to the support for Greece, which in turn focused advisors to seek political moderation within Greek politics.[82] America was willing to help, but only if Greece based its ideals on a free and inclusive form of governance that would prove to the Greek people its legitimacy and therefore gain their support.

Dean Acheson, the assistant Secretary of State to George Marshall, initially estimated only forty military advisors were needed and those estimates were based on a hope that although Britain was pulling out its military forces it would retain its advisory corps of several hundred. The first components of United States Army Group in Greece (USAGG) arrived just two days after congressional approval.[83]

43

The USAGG was initially slightly larger than Dean Acheson's estimation to Congress, at fifty-four officers, soldiers and civilians, and the Navy contingent added an additional thirty men. The State Department, which would supervise the aid program, contributed a staff of seventy personnel in Washington, DC, under George McGhee, and delegated another eighty-nine personnel to liaison with the other departments. Both the forward deployed and the Washington based sections would ultimately be responsible to the chief of the American Mission in Greece, Dwight Griswold, a former Republican governor of Nebraska who served with Truman in World War I and was at the time working in the American military government in Germany.[84] Although USAGG did not bring any ―boots on the ground‖ it did bring wings in the air. The most decisive support that Washington brought to the besieged Greek military came in the form of airpower.

The Royal Hellenic Air Force (RHAF) at its height numbered no more than 7,500 airmen and pilots. The estimated cost of the air campaign was approximately ten percent of the ground campaign. It was the last of the Greek service branches to get established and take part in the war. This was primarily because of the lack of an industrial base which precluded qualified pilots and mechanics. Britain and the United States not only had to provide the planes, armament, munitions and training for the pilots, but the training for all of the support personnel. The person put in charge of this herculean task was Brigadier General William A. Matheny, United States Air Force (USAF), who arrived in Greece in February 1948.[85]

Both the United States and Great Britain provided planes. USAFE (United States Air Force Europe) provided C-47 and AT-6 aircraft immediately, while British Spitfires were shipped from the United Kingdom. Although the initial aircraft were operational in early 1948, they were not suited for loitering to provide close air support. The Spitfire, although a capable fighter did not have a long range, carried limited ammunition and needed to re-zero its machined guns for the ground attack role. The C-47 transports from USAFE had great range and to capitalize on this, the RHAF modified them to carry 250 and 500 pound bombs on racks beneath the fuselage. This was later abandoned because the poor accuracy of bombing with a cargo plane was quickly realized.[86]

The RHAF conducted both battlefield isolation missions and direct support of ground forces. Three techniques for battlefield isolation were pre-planned strikes based on intelligence or aerial photography; armed reconnaissance; and spotting by reconnaissance planes who would then call in bombers and fighter-bombers to attack troop formations, supply caches, or fixed fortifications. Limited artillery pieces and the mountainous terrain prevented the Greek military from employing large numbers of field artillery. Just as Germany realized the advantages of the Stuka bomber during the Blitzkrieg, Greek generals adopted the RHAF as a mobile artillery platform. In an attempt to directly support the ground forces, the Greek military used vehicle mounted radios at the brigade and division levels and later developed ―mule pack air support signal units" down to lower levels. Lack of combined arms training and limited signals due to mountainous terrain prevented good ground to air coordination throughout the war.[87]

Another critical part to the successful defeat of the insurgency within Greece was on the political front. With the United States' involvement came some expectations of the Greek government to reform into a more democratic form that would represent all the people. In the summer of 1947, a new government was formed in Athens that elected a moderate liberal Themistoklis Sophoulis. Under Sophoulis' leadership the Greek government contained people from all the major parties within Greece, giving it a legitimate platform and taking away a major propaganda tool of the KKE.[88] The Greek prime minister was willing and sought to steer his Athens based government toward an ―ultimate aim‖ shared by Washington. He wanted to lift security measures as soon as possible and broaden government to include all parties that were loyal to a free, democratic Greece. In return he expected the promised American immediate and long term aid. Underscoring Greece's dire situation, Ambassador Lincoln MacVeagh wrote to Secretary of State George C. Marshall, ―The main obstacle to the success of these efforts of mine has always been the difficult economic and financial condition of the country.‖[89] Along with the aid he asked for a ―timely increase of the Greek armed forces,‖ so that they could quickly defeat Communist insurgent forces.[90] This new found legitimacy was backed up by a United Nations inspection team sent by the Security Council which concluded that not only were Greece's northern neighbors supporting an insurgency in hopes of gaining territory, but that ―Greece, especially in Athens and Salonika,‖ offered substantial ―political freedom, freedom of speech, press, and assembly.‖[91]

To counter these latest moves the guerilla movement announced a provisional government ―somewhere in the mountains of northern Greece.‖[92] To coincide with this political announcement, the military arm of the Communist Party ordered an attack on the town of Konista. The persistent attacks to seize a capitol cost the Democratic Army of Greece (DAG) heavily. The battle raged for eight days, but when government reinforcements arrived in the area on 1 January 1948, the ELAS fighters admitted defeat by the much larger and better armed Greek military. Significant for this engagement was the tactics used by the Communist guerillas. For the first time during the war they fought

46

as a conventional force against the Greek army and were soundly defeated. Some 650 dead and wounded guerilla fighters were left on the battlefield by the retreating Communists.[93]

With some success in the political and military spheres, and money, equipment, and advice pouring in from the United States, divisions in the Communist camp might very well have put the final nail in the coffin of the Greek Communist Party. Although Tito hoped to gain stature and possibly territory by providing large amounts of support for the Communist guerillas, Stalin had not only made an agreement with Britain over the splitting of areas of influence but was also genuinely concerned about the United States' involvement. Stalin told Bulgarian and Yugoslav Communists in 1948, —The uprising in Greece must be stopped, and as quickly as possible." Fearing they had no chance of success, Stalin rhetorically asked, —what do you think . . . that Great Britain and the United States--the United States, the most powerful state in the world--will permit you to break their lines of communication in the Mediterranean Sea?"[94] Additionally, Moscow was not happy with Tito putting his federation of Slavic states together.

In 1949, Tito's ally in the Greek Communist Party, Markos Vafiades, was relieved from his position as head of the Democratic Army of Greece. The KKE then sided with the Soviet Union and supported a free and independent Macedonia, threatening Tito's dream of a Slavic federation. In response to this, Tito shut off his borders to the Greek Communists. Although they still received limited support from Albania and Bulgaria, this support was insufficient for the Communist guerillas to continue against an increasingly powerful Greek military funded and equipped by the United States.[95]

47

Both sides of the war played a part in the final result of the fighting. The Communist insurgency became a victim of its own success. Having done so well up to 1948, along with overreaction on the part of the Greek government, the guerilla forces swelled in numbers. But as the Democratic Army reorganized into a more conventional type force, it negated its advantages of speed, flexibility and security. Lacking combined arms and unable to fight the conventional fight, the Communist fighters played right into the Greek government forces' advantages of being able to mass infantry, artillery and fighter bombers onto the Communist formations.[96]

[1]Edgar O'Ballance, *The Greek Civil War, 1944-1949* (New York: Praeger, 1966), 19.

[2]George Andrew Kourvetaris, "Professional Self-images and Political Perspectives in the Greek Military," *American Sociological Review*, 36 (1971): 1043-57.

[3]Andre Gerolymatos, *Red Acropolis, Black Terror: The Greek Civil War and the Origins of Soviet-American Rivalry, 1943-1949* (New York: Basic Books, 2004). 1-4.

[4]Richard Clogg, *A Concise History of Greece* (Cambridge: Cambridge University Press, 1992), 100.

[5]Ibid., 18-20.

[6]O'Ballance, *Greek Civil War*, 27-31.

[7]Ibid., 13.

[8]*Red Acropolis, Black Terror*, 54-55.

[9]Glenn E. Curtis, *Greece: A Country Study* (Washington, DC: Government Printing Office, 1995), 85.

[10]Ibid., 85-88.

[11]O'Ballance, *Greek Civil War*, 21.

[12]Curtis, *Greece: A Country Study*, 56-57; O'Ballance, *Greek Civil War*, 55.

[13]O'Ballance, *The Greek Civil War*, 20-21.

[14]Ibid., 27.

[15]Clogg, *A Concise History of Greece*, 47-48.

[16]O'Ballance, *Greek Civil War*, 27.

[17]Clogg, *A Concise History of Greece*, 81-86.

[18]Ibid., 114.

[19]O'Ballance, *Greek Civil War*, 28.

[20]Clogg, *A Short History of Modern Greece*, 117-118.

[21]Jon Van der Kiste, *Kings of the Hellenes* (Gloucestershire, 1994), 144.

[22]O'Ballance, *Greek Civil War*, 29.

[23]D. George Kousoulas, *Revolution and Defeat* (London: Oxford University Press, 1965), 3-5.

[24]O'Ballance, *Greek Civil War*, 29.

[25]Kousoulas, *Revolution and Defeat*, 8-9.

[26]Ibid., 106-112. Metaxas fled Greece with King George II, after the failures at Smyrna.

[27]Ibid., 115-117.

[28]Clogg, *A Short History of Modern Greece*, 130-132.

[29]Curtis, *Greece: A Country Study*, 236.

[30]O'Ballance, *Greek Civil War*, 31.

[31]Ibid., 13.

[32]Clogg, *A Short History of Modern Greece*, 133-136.

[33]Correspondence with Dr. House Manuscript, 1 of Chapter 1.

[34]Helen Chapin Metz, ed., *Turkey: A Country Study,* (1995), 39.

[35]Stephanos Zotos, *Greece: The Struggle for Freedom* (New York: Cromwell Company, 1967), 2-5.

[36]O'Ballance, *Greek Civil War*, 33.

[37]Gerhard L. Weinberg, *A World At Arms: A Global History of World War II,* (Cambridge: Cambridge University Press, 1994), 142-149.

[38]Zotos, *Greece: The Struggle for Freedom,* 78-81.

[39]O'Ballance, *Greek Civil War,* 53-55.

[40]Haris Vlavianos, *Greece, 1941-49: From Resistance to Civil War* (New York: St. Martin's Press,1992), 18.

[41]Vlavianos, *Greece,* 18, 19. Quotations on both pages.

[42]Ibid., 25-28.

[43]O'Ballance, *Greek Civil War,* 53-57.

[44]Ibid., 57-64.

[45]Dimitrios G. Kousoulas, *The Price of Freedom* (Syracuse, NY: Syracuse University Press, 1953), 99.

[46]Vlavianos, *Greece, 1941-49: From Resistance to Civil War,* 34.

[47]Kousoulas, *The Price of Freedom,* 111-113.

[48]Curtis, *Greece: A Country Study,* 61.

[49]Zotos, *Greece: The Struggle for Freedom,* 148-149.

[50]Ibid., 149-151.

[51]Curtis, *Greece: A Country Study,* 61-62.

[52]E. W. Downs, M. A. Campbell, and L. V. Schuetta, ―The Employment of Airpower in the Greek Guerilla War, 1947-1949," Concepts Division, U.S. Aerospace Studies Institute, ed., *Air Studies* (1964), 2.

[53]Curtis, *Greece: A Country Study,* 62.

[54]John O. Iatrides, ―Greece at the Crossroads, 1944-1950", John O. Iatrides and Linda Wrigley, ed., *Greece at the Crossroads: The Civil War and Its Legacy* (University Park: PA: 1995), 1-30, 15-16.

[55]Kousoulas, *Revolution and Defeat,* 197.

[56]Iatrides, ―Greece At the Crossroads," 16.

[57]Eugen J. Aslanis, ―Guerilla War in Greece: 1946-1949," (1968), 6-7.

[58]Zotos, *Greece: The Struggle for Freedom*, 167-68.

[59]John O. Iatrides, ―Greece at the Crossroads, 1944-1950," *Greece at the Crossroads: The Civil War and Its Legacy*, ed. John O. Iatrides and Linda Wrigley, (University Park, PA: The Pennsylvania State University Press, 1995), 14.

[60]Zotos, *Greece: The Struggle for Freedom*, 157-161.

[61]Ibid., 169.

[62]M. A. Campbell, Downs, et al., ―The Employment of Airpower in the Greek Guerilla War, 1947-1949," 16-17, 62.

[63]O'Ballance, *Greek Civil War*, 14.

[64]Downs et al., ―The Employment of Airpower in the Greek Guerilla War, 1947-1949", 16-19.

[65]Howard Jones, *A New Kind of War: America's Global Strategy and The Truman Doctrine in Greece,* (Oxford: 1989), 64.

[66]Downs et al., ―The Employment of Airpower in the Greek Guerilla War, 1947-1949," 23-24.

[67]Dr. House's manuscript, Chapter 1 page 1 from correspondence.

[68]Zotos, *Greece: The Struggle for Freedom*, 152-156.

[69]S. Everett Gleason, "Foreign Relations of the United States, 1947: The near East and Africa," ed. U.S. Department of State, Foreign Relations of the United States (Washington, DC: Government Printing Press, 1973), 532.

[70]Jones, *A New Kind of War: America's Global Strategy and The Truman Doctrine in Greece*, 43.

[71]Ibid., 43.

[72]Ibid., 43.

[73]Ibid., 45-51, quote on 45.

[74]Ibid., 47.

[75]Ibid., 48, 61.

[76]Ibid., 47-50.

[77]Ibid., 60.

[78] Ibid., 61.

[79] Ibid.

[80] Lawrence S. Wittner, *American Intervention in Greece, 1943-1949* (New York, 1982), 76-77.

[81] Ibid.

[82] Ibid., 78.

[83] Lawrence S. Wittner, *American Intervention in Greece, 1943-1949* (New York, 1982), 224.

[84] Jones, *A New Kind of War: America's Global Strategy and The Truman Doctrine in Greece*, 60-62.

[85] Downs, et al., —The Employment of Airpower in the Greek Guerilla War, 1947-1949," 34, 58.

[86] Ibid., 35, 36.

[87] Ibid., 37-38.

[88] Zotos, *Greece: The Struggle for Freedom*, 173.

[89] S. Everett Gleason, —Foreign Relations of the United States, 1947: The Near East and Africa," U.S. Department of State, ed., (1973), 7.

[90] S. Everett Gleason, —Foreign Relations of the United States, 1947: The Near East and Africa", U.S. Department of State, ed., (1973), 7.

[91] Zotos, *Greece: The Struggle for Freedom*, 173-174.

[92] Kousoulas, *Revolution and Defeat*, 224.

[93] Ibid.

[94] Ibid.

[95] Zotos, *Greece: The Struggle for Freedom*, 178-180.

[96] Downs et al., —The Employment of Airpower in the Greek Guerilla War, 1947-1949," 20.

CHAPTER 3

OMAN

There are enclaves of the world where, due to their customs and religion, the people cling to tradition. In some cases their traditions are more important than the pull toward embracing technological advancement and improvements that the Western world would associate with progress. Because of this draw toward tradition, inhabitants of these regions tend to stick with the ways of the old and let the rest of the world go by them. For one reason or another, industrial or informational improvements that bring prosperity and knowledge in developed areas around the world bypass these areas. Culture and religion play a part in determining this phenomenon, but inevitably resources and strategic location play a more definitive role. Thomas Barnett calls these technologically deprived enclaves gap countries or regions.[1] The rest of the world continues to move forward at a blistering pace and these countries, sometimes for lack of strategic importance, fail to progress with technological advancements. They fail to be a part of the global community. Eventually, however, despite the efforts of their political or religious leaders, the global community finds them. Just such an occurrence happened in the small Persian Gulf country of Oman.

Already important for its location at the choke point of the Persian Gulf and Indian Ocean, Oman's strategic importance manifested during the boom of oil exploration in the early 20th century (see Appendix B for timeline). Oil was found in Oman in 1962 and the country started drilling and exporting oil products by 1967.[2] Despite Sultan Sa'id ibn Taimur granting oil concessions in his country as early as 1937 and his ties with Great Britain, he was an isolationist. He feared not only outsiders, but those of his countrymen that had visited the West and tried to bring back Western technologies and ideas. Even upon his own son's return from Britain's Royal Military

Academy at Sandhurst, the Sultan placed the young man under virtual house arrest and kept him away from politics.[3] The Sultan only tolerated the occasional visit from other rulers or dignitaries. Although the Sultan was a wise man, he was not educated in the ways of the West and was ignorant about technological advancements in farming, oil and other industries.[4] As far as the Sultan was concerned, medicine, technology and education were means of subversion and he was afraid that bringing such advancements into his country would pervert his people from their religion and culture. Initial lack of development could be explained away since Oman was a poor country, but when oil revenues started making the Sultan a very rich man, his lavish expenditures on his palace, vehicles and royal yacht caused animosity amongst the Omani people that eventually turned into open rebellion, insurgency and war.[5]

Although it is difficult to truly measure the size of these desert states, Oman is approximately 212,000 square kilometers of desert, mountains and coastal plains. While most of the country is desert, about 15 percent is mountainous. The country is divided into four major regions: Musandam Peninsula, Al Batinah coastal plain, Oman interior, and the focus of this chapter--the fight over Dhofar Region (see Figure 5. Map of Oman on page 53 and Figure 6. Map of Dhofar Region on page 58). Oman borders the United Arab Emirates, Saudi Arabia and Yemen and most critically for its strategic importance in the global community, the Musandam Peninsula juts out into the Strait of Hormuz where most of the world's oil floats by in giant ships. By the end of the rebellion in 1975 there were approximately 450,000 people living in Oman, of which only 50,000 were from the Dhofar Region.[6]

What makes Oman different from many of the very arid Persian Gulf states dates back to the time of the Persian occupation of the region 2,500 years ago, when the Falaj (underground channel) system was dug, creating a length of oases the whole distance end to end of the plain that extends along the span of the country. This, along with the rainfall from the southwest monsoon that covers the country from June to September each year, makes parts of Oman, especially the Dhofar region, very fertile with constant running streams in some places.[7]

The area where most of the fighting took place was made up of rugged mountainous ranges that rose as high as 5,500 feet over the Indian Ocean. As what seems to be the case in many mountainous areas, the people in the Jebal are very independent and, especially at the time of the insurgency, were separated from the rest of their countrymen. The Jebal Akhdar, also known as the "camel's hideout" in northern Oman, was the scene of intensive fighting during the Jebal Akhdar War between 1957-1959. Only 130 of the 1,500 square kilometers of Dhofar are affected by the monsoons.[8] But the changes in that affected area are dramatic.

When looking at it from about 150 kilometers up, the dark brown formation of mountains that catch the cloud formations and their precious water look like a giant semi-circle. From mid June to late September dense cloud formations cover these mountains to as low as 650 feet elevation. During these summer months, the climate can be described as "muddy, cold and insect ridden."[9] This cold, wet climate and the runoff from the limestone mountain ranges cause deep ravines and heavy thick vegetation in an otherwise dry desert area. Further east on the mountain range, the wadis grow deeper and wild figs and lime trees along with lianas, which is a type of ground cover, grow in

56

abundance. This vegetation gave excellent concealment to the insurgents even during the dry season of October to June. Further up the mountain ranges, incense trees grow of which the bark was a source of income for the nomads in that region up until about 1970. Along the southern slopes of the eastern ranges, small fields and lower rainfall permit a limited agrarian existence. The Jebalis, local tribal inhabitants of the Jebal, raise cattle, camels and goats and grow beans and tobacco.[10] Beyond the plains of the coastline the elevation rises and the area not affected by the monsoons is a high rocky desert. The whole area formidably high and difficult made the land difficult for government forces to traverse up unnoticed, and insurgents could either choose to fight the approaching forces or flee away easily into one of the many mountain passes.[11]

The country had a very tumultuous past. Almost every village had a fort. Some were significant in size and some were still being used when the British came in the 1960s to help the Sultan defeat the communist insurgency.[12] The origins of many of Oman's challenges in the mid 20th century originated with Sultan Sa'id bin Taimur. The Sultan was from the Muscat Province of northern Oman and married a Dhofari woman, who gave birth to the Sultan's son, Qaboos. He loved the Dhofar area so much he spent the last ten years of his rule there in Salalah, despite the capital of his country being Muscat in northern Oman. This caused some animosity between the rich northern Omani tribes and the Sultan for there was also no love lost between northern Oman and southern Oman.[13] A northern Omani saying went that —if your path is blocked by a snake and a Dhofari, kill the Dhofari first.‖[14] But if one subscribes to Machiavelli's philosophy of a ruler living in his conquered land, the Sultan's residence and, more importantly, his son Qaboos' residence in Dhofar placed him in the perfect location to allow him to maintain control over a province that was very different from the Muscat region from which the Sultan's family originated.[15]

The Omani culture was very different from that of the British advisors helping them in the counterinsurgency. The British soldier coming into this culture learned not from books but from immersion into the Omani society. In an illiterate society like Oman, stories are used as a means to pass on culture, history and morals. Some of the stories were fascinating and stuck with the British visitors for the rest of their lives. The Omani villagers often told Ian Gardiner, a British Royal Marine who fought in Dhofar from 1973 to 1975, of the *djinns* or evil spirits that lived in the small whirlwinds of sand or dust. If one was caught in such little tornadoes they could be possessed by the evil spirits.[16]

Other very non-western practices that take part in Oman might catch the unprepared advisor off guard. For example, medical techniques used by the Omanis were rudimentary and sometimes practically medieval as compared to the British. One of the accepted practices was based on their belief that pain should be treated with more pain. For example, if a child complained about an ailment such as a headache, the treatment more often than not was a red hot poker or knife applied to the arm.[17] A surprisingly beneficial result to this was that simple Western drugs such as aspirin that had never been taken by the Dhofari people had very positive medicinal effects.[18]

Living in a very harsh country that did not have what Westerners would term normal jobs, industry or even an education system made it a difficult or unfamiliar concept for Omani men to see exerting themselves beyond survival as being worthwhile to gain improvement in their daily lives. From their viewpoint, they need only to work just hard enough to maintain an adequate subsistence for them and their families. Industrious work efforts beyond subsistence farming that might offer great rewards to Americans or Europeans did not offer the similar rewards to Omani men especially under the old Sultan and therefore did not fit within the Omani culture.[19] This clashed with the Protestant work ethic brought by the Englishmen and initial efforts to motivate their local counterparts left many British officers frustrated. Had it not been for the special character of those chosen to advise local Omani forces, which will be discussed in more detail later, many successes that were achieved might have been undone by frustrated acts of lesser quality British soldiers.

Along with a different work ethic in Oman came a different sense of leadership and followership. The Omani tribal system is very democratic in that anyone within the tribe has the right to decide and argue their fate. As a result, when an order to execute a mission was given to Dhofari tribesmen, they thought it was completely within their rights to decide when, if and where they were going to attack the enemy. So what at first looked like indiscipline and poor followership to the British advisors, who initially failed to understand local culture, was in actuality the Dhofari men arguing their expected opinions as they had been doing all of their lives.[20] Although anyone could voice his opinions there was another leadership aspect that saved advisors significant amounts of time and energy. The tribal sheikh had almost absolute power over the people of his tribe, thus winning over the sheikh in a sense meant winning over large numbers of people.[21]

Although Oman is a Muslim country it has several different sects of Islam with the primary sect being Ibadi. In the Ibadi religion the religious scholars select a leader that can best defend the community and rule according to Islamic principles. While there are also differences in both Shia and Sunni sects of Islam, the primary difference in Ibadi was that the Imam was the defender of the community. Another major difference within the Ibadi is that they believe they are different from the other sects because they are strict in their interpretation of the Kuran and therefore are the true followers of Islam. They refer to themselves as ―the Muslims or the people of straightness (ahl al-istiqama)".[22] British observers of this sect state that it is the least sectarian and many Ibadi will openly pray with outsiders. Their religion only calls for them on a personal level to dissociate with non-believers. In the Ibadi Islamic faith only hostile action is needed against the unjust ruler.[23] These differences in the Ibadi beliefs expectedly led to some seclusion between Oman's Ibadi sect and that of the rest of the Islamic world. Although Persia was an Islamic state while it occupied coastal cities in Oman during part of the first and second millennium, Persians would not let the Ibadi religious sect of Islam affect their trade along the coast. As a result Oman has always been somewhat divided between the mountainous region controlled by the Ibadi and the coastal plains.[24]

Oman is the only state within the Persian Gulf to be ruled by a sultan instead of a sheikh.[25] By his very title the Sultan of Oman is more a secular leader then a religious one. While Ahmad ibn Sa'id, the first of the Sa'id ruling family, was originally named Imam by the Ibadis after casting out the Persian rulers in the 18th century, his son Sa'id ibn Ahmad Al Sa'id, was the only other Sa'id ruler to receive religious approval for succession as Imam. After Sa'id ibn Ahmad Al Sa'id, all other Sa'id rulers called themselves sultans. The Sa'id family further removed their religious associations to power by moving the capital from Ar Rustaq, the traditional Ibadi religious center, to Muscat along the coast.[26] This caused tensions between the Islamic leadership and the ruling family which, when pushed by outside forces mainly the Ottoman Empire, Saudi Arabia and Egypt, caused the Imam of Oman to rally the interior tribes against the Sultan, first in 1895 and again in 1913. With support of the Indian and British government forces, the Sultan was able to defeat the rebellion in 1915 at the Battle of Bayt al-Falaj, but it was not until 1920 that a peace treaty was agreed upon between the Sultan and the Imamate (office of the Imam).[27] This break between the Sultan and the Ibadi Islamic leadership could be used as fuel by insurgent forces initially in the Dhofar insurgency since most of the Jebalis were devout Ibadi Muslims.

An interesting paradox on the religious fervor of the interior tribes that caused the Sultan difficulty would also cause a rift in the later insurgency. The difference between the Jebali's Islamic faith and the atheist s who assisted them in their insurgency against the Sultan in the 1960s and 1970s caused significant strains that would eventually cause many Jebalis to join the side of the Sultan. Such atrocities as fathers being forced to offer their daughters to the fighters as their -duty to the Front" and the atheist s cutting the noses off and blinding of old men who refused to deny Allah caused many -hard-core members" of the original Dhofar Liberation Front to walk off the Jebal and surrender to the Sultan.[28]

The Omanis' devotion to God, however, would cause some frustration in their Western advisors. British soldiers found that Islam caused a fatalistic feeling within the Omanis. Muslims, following their faith, surrender to -God's will" and therefore everything that happens is by his doing, not their own. A common phrase in Oman used throughout the Arab world today was -Insh Allah." When asked or prodded to get the Omanis to try harder or make a difference in something, they would reply, *Insh Allah*: God willing.[29] Although initially frustrated, the British leaders and advisors eventually learned to work within and around such fatalistic approaches in order to lead the host national forces to victory.

Since World War II the Gulf Region has become a strategic location. The Musandam Peninsula which lies along the Strait of Hormuz, although separated by the United Arab Emirates, is a province of Oman (see Figure 5. Map of Oman on page 53).

Although authorities disagree with exactly how much crude oil flows through the strait, it is undisputable how much the world's industrialized nations depend on the precious resource that flows by Oman's separated province.[30] The Gulf Cooperation Council (GCC), of which Oman is a member, is similar to the North Atlantic Treaty Organization. It is a loose affiliation of Gulf States that focuses on the protection of the member states. Although showing weakness in defending Kuwait during the Iraq Invasion in 1990, the council realized the importance of the strait and devotes air and naval assets as well as training funds in the coalition efforts to prepare for the defense of the strait in case of attack.[31]

Interestingly enough, most of the people that fought in the Dhofar insurgency never laid eyes on this strategic waterway. Even though Dhofar is over 600 kilometers to the south of the strategic peninsula, British authorities understood that if the sultan fell to insurgents, the flow of oil could easily be threatened. Furthermore, since the end of World War II the British were involved in a series of colonial conflicts, entwined within the context of a larger Cold War strategy against communist forces.[32] British forces were spread around the world involved in everything from major counterinsurgency operations in South East Asia to protecting Western Europe from the threat of the Soviet horde massed to the east. To compound the matter, Britain never focused on maintaining a large conventional army so they simply did not have the troops for the type of fight that was coming. They were even less interested in committing troops to the type of war that Sir Robert Thompson described as being "a long, arduous and protracted struggle."[33] So instead British military leaders, possibly inadvertently, provided the exact type of troop structure needed to win such a war.

The British forces within Oman can only be described as a hodgepodge. Although the Sultan's Armed Forces (SAF) did not officially form until 1958, British officers have fought in the service of the Sultan since Indian troops supported the defeat of the Ibadi Imam's forces in 1915.[34] This relationship of British officers leading Omani troops was formalized during the Imam's revolt in northern Oman in the late 1950s. On July 25, 1958, Sultan Sa'id bin Taimur wrote a personal letter to British Undersecretary of State Julian Amery, in which he discussed the agreement between himself and the British Crown, agreeing to use Regular British Army officers on what was termed "secondment."[35] They would lead the SAF from that point until the 1980s. In some cases these officers would retire from the British Army and spend years in the SAF. Other British officers and senior non-commissioned officers would take a year leave of absence from the British Army or Royal Marines and work, usually at a higher pay grade with the benefits of the higher rank, in the SAF before returning to their former rank and position within the British military. The only difference between the two was that the former was paid directly by the Sultan while the British seconded officers who were on leave from the British military for one year were still paid from their own government.[36]

Although the number of British seconded soldiers would fluctuate from year to year, there were never more than a couple of hundred officers in the SAF at any one time. For example, in 1964 a total of 52 British officers were in the SAF.[37] While these numbers were low, the positions held were at all levels of command up to the very highest levels of the SAF. British officers under an Omani Deputy Defense Minister held the positions of Commander of SAF (CSAF), Commander Sultan of Oman's Navy (CSON), Commander Sultan of Oman's Air Force (CSOAF) and Commander of the

Dhofar Brigade. They also held most of the battalion and company commands within the Omani force as well.[38]

Lacking educated officers in such things as aviation and artillery, the Sultan initially relied heavily on contracted foreign personnel to conduct the technical jobs within his military. British pilots from the Royal Air Force (RAF) were eventually contracted to fly for the Sultan's of Oman's Air Force (SOAF).[39] As the insurgency increased in violence and depth, the elite 22nd Special Air Service Regiment (SAS) was committed along with the previous British contingent to the fight. Initially under the acronym BATT, which stood for British Army Training Teams, the first full SAS troop went to Oman in 1970 and the first full SAS squadron was on the ground training, leading and fighting with local national forces in 1971.[40]

British advisors had to endure many of the same conditions and deprivations of their Omani soldiers.[41] Although having such niceties as access to a pool when they were in the north of Oman and out of combat, they learned to deal with the extreme heat that rose to above 122 degrees Fahrenheit. The heat affected British officer Ian Gardiner so much, he was completely incapacitated the first time he went on a practice mission. However, like their counterparts they learned to work early in the morning from six to nine and after a short breakfast at nine o'clock they would resume work until one o'clock in the afternoon. At this time of the day the heat became unbearable and, although some events might cause them to work during this part of the day, on the average they avoided doing any hard labor.[42]

British advisors and commanders learned to use the same type of Arabic latrine which consisted of nothing more than a hole in the floor. Although far different from

65

what the British soldiers were accustomed, this crude system was quite out of necessity in an environment that was short on water. Another local method of using one's hand instead of toilet paper also had to be learned. No doubt due to the stench of the latrines and the desire to use toilet paper, soldiers at first chose a spot outside the barracks or they would use rocks to clean themselves the best they could then toss the stones down the hole in the floor. As they got used to the latrines and the Arab way to clean with water instead of using toilet paper, the smelly landmines around the barracks area disappeared and the toilets were no longer fouled up with paper and rocks.[43] Other nuances were easier to stomach.

British officers fighting in Oman were always being invited to eat with their Omani companions and therefore had to learn the local way of eating meals. They knew that to refuse food or drink from their hosts was a huge insult and instead of feigning being full or picking around the edges, the men drank and ate, at times, very unpalatable meals with a smile on their face and a –Shukran", meaning thank you, to follow.[44] They also came to appreciate what was initially a very foreign meal of goat and rice. Although not used to sharing from a communal platter, they learned to take pleasure in understanding the deeper meaning behind this eating style. Inviting a person into one's home to share a meal was a welcoming sign of respect and friendship. Better situational understanding allowed them to realize little nuances such as what was left on the platter after the invited guests were done eating was given to the lower enlisted or the women and the children in a family. This ensured that they did not eat too much and, if they happened to not like the food in front of them, it gave them an easy out, by politely stating that they were leaving the rest of the food for the others.[45] In the Arab world one squats appropriately on the rug during their communal meals. They do this carefully to not show the soles of their feet in order to not offend their hosts. As with other customs British officers, although painful at first, learned to squat with their feet folded up underneath them like it was second nature.[46]

British officers within the employment of the Sultan would wear the uniform of that army. Their work uniform consisted of an olive green shirt and the same colored denim pants. This attempt to fit in was for their soldiers' sake as well as for their own protection. British officers were primary targets to the enemy insurgents, but despite their height and pale skin, some would blend in quite well. Many of the officers within the Sultan's army, after a deepening tan and a closely cropped beard, became unrecognizable to the foreigner's eye. On one occurrence when a senior British officer attempted to talk to one of the Sultan's soldiers in his practiced Arabic, the soldier responded in Arabic to his questions. It was not until later that the visiting dignitary realized that he was talking to Arthur Brocklehurst, the British Regimental second in command. Other soldiers would wear a dishdasha off duty, because they learned that in this very hot climate such an outfit is more practical leisure wear than pants because it lets air flow better around the body.[47]

As well as learning the language and being mindful of the culture, British advisors were very careful about dealing with the intricacies of the Muslim religion. Instead of just expecting soldiers to fight and soldier on through the holy month of Ramadan, the Qhadhi, the senior cleric responsible for interpretation of Sharia law, was sought to give permission for Islamic local national soldiers to fight, eat and drink normally through Ramadan while deployed into the combat zone. They were careful to include in the

67

request to the Qadhi that the Muslim would be fighting an atheist, which was at least partially true. The Qadhi, no doubt glad to be asked, responded that it was the duty of the soldiers to fight and that if he died during Ramadan he would be a martyr despite not having met the requirements during Ramadan. The devout Muslim fighter could make up his responsibilities at a later date if needed.[48] Another factor of religion caught British officers off guard during initial missions onto the Jebal. Although they realized that devout Muslims stopped five times a day and faced Mecca to say their prayers, they never expected them to do it in the middle of an ambush. After delicately explaining the dangers, most Omani soldiers saved prayer for the base camps.[49]

The most important factor to realize about the British military force was that the very low numbers of British soldiers allowed for the very best to be there. Those that served in the SAF were volunteers, handpicked not only by senior British officials, but ultimately the Sultan himself.[50] Although the British SAS served as a British unit in Oman, the very nature of the British SAS ensured that any who served in the force were already elite. This is the exact type of force that was needed to adapt to a very different and challenging environment. Although most Englishmen serving were not fluent in Arabic, they would do their best to learn the language needed to converse with the host nation soldiers.[51] There was no air of superiority among the officers when dealing with the host national forces; humility was sacrosanct.[52] The British did not limit themselves to the duties required of an officer. Most conducted the functions of a sergeant major or lower enlisted. This was not because they did not trust the Omani NCOs, or consider them incompetent, but because most were illiterate or could not speak English.[53]

68

Having volunteered for this sort of work, these soldiers were far less likely to cause any incidents disrespectful to the Omani culture or religion. These incidents sometimes weaken or negate any good that is done and can be devastating to a counterinsurgency where the center of gravity is almost always with the hearts and minds of the local populous. This type of positive, culturally accepting and mission focused attitude also generated a feeling of unity of effort. The British officers and SAS soldiers fought not just in the same battles, but along side of their Omani counterparts.[54] They were not two different units out on the battlefield fighting a coalition. They were one force with one common goal fighting under the command of the civilian leadership of the Dhofar Development Committee and the Sultan himself.

There was very little medical care within the country and many of the Omanis had no dental care as well. There was a hospital in Muscat and some clinics in the bigger towns, but many locals just went without care unless it was an emergency. The British medical personnel, when they were not patching up their own men from combat, spent their time among the population providing what medical help they could.[55] These medical orderlies were called *campowda* which stood for –compounder of medicines," and British advisers took the *campowda* with them whenever they did their rounds to treat the locals' maladies. The injuries and ailments would range from the all too common eye infection to more serious disease and injury such as tuberculosis or broken bones. In many cases all that could be given was aspirin, but even aspirin seemed to have amazing effects on the people. In order to treat so many people often the British medical officers would set up and run regular clinics.[56]

This effort was not seen as secondary or tertiary to the main mission. This is seen best when looking at the British SAS' three step insurgency plan in Oman. The initial aim was to —bing immediate relief to the people." The second aim was to —train the Omanis to take over these measures" themselves. The long term solution was that —everything that goes into the makeup of a modern state," to include Oman's infrastructure and security was in the hands of Oman's government. That third step defined success or mission accomplishment.[57]

The war in southern Oman had global strategic implications. Although small in size, the war also had global as well as local origins. Initially the local problem developed from disaffection with the rule of Sultan Sa'id bin Taimur.[58] As young Dhofari men went out into the world and saw the advances in technology and individual rights that were not offered to them in their home country, they became frustrated with the Sultan's rule.[59] Just as the Sultan had feared, they brought that disaffection home with them. There were numerous opposition groups that arose or migrated to Oman's front door.[60] The catalyst for actual armed conflict was a small incident where one of his local askaris, a civilian guard, arrested local Musallim bin Nufal bin Sharfan al-Kathiri of the powerful Bayt Kathir Tribe for riding a bicycle into town. Hostilities started in April of 1963 when Musallim and a couple of his family members attacked an oil company truck on its way back to the company camp in the Jebal. Initially the townspeople of Salalah, Dhofar's provincial capital, were vocal against the Sultan and gave some support to the dissidents, but the actual armed aggression originated from the Jebal. Although Musallim was able to recruit a few members from his area, most of his tribe did not support his activities, but were also unwilling to give information to the government.[61]

The lack of willingness to give information to the government forces in Dhofar contributed to an unclear enemy situation which in turn caused the Sultan's frustrated forces to indiscriminately attack areas within the region. Such punitive raids by the Sultan's forces within Dhofar had the unsurprising effect of bringing more Dhofari people, especially the Jebalis, to the side of the insurgency.[62] As the insurgents grew from a few men to as many as four hundred or more fighters, the Oman conflict popped up on the world's radar and other countries became involved in the fight. Either from ideological positions resulting from the Cold War dogmas or from longstanding animosities or alliances, countries around the world chose sides. Men from Jordan, Iran, India, Pakistan and Britain fought on the side of the Sultan, while others from Yemen, Russia, Libya, Cuba and China fought on the side of the insurgency.[63] Other countries that did not send men contributed in other ways. For example, many of the Dhofar rebels received training in Iraq.

In June of 1965 rebel forces held a conference in al-Wadi al-Kabir where all the disparate elements fighting against the Sultan unified under the Dhofar Liberation Front (DLF). In 1966 the Dhofar Liberation Army (DLA) was named and small units of men started training and fighting together. Except in a few circumstances, like the attack on Mirbat, these elements did not function in more than platoon size elements of twenty or so men. However, they could be called on by radio to gather in larger numbers when needed.[64] Such disparate arrangements similar to coalitions are tough to hold together, and Musallim bin Nufal had lost favor with supporters outside Oman as well as the Imam of Oman. As the DLF continued to lose battles and support from inside and outside Oman, they joined forces with an unlikely group.

The Peoples' Front for the Liberation of Occupied Arabian Gulf (PFLOAG), later called the Peoples' Front for the Liberation of Oman (PFLO), was strongly communist. In 1967 the insurgent group took control of British controlled Aden, causing Britain to abandon the country.[65] China and the Soviet Union supported the organization from Yemen and later Aden in the form of weapons, money and training. Although initially the DLF did not support such a godless organization, the amount of money and weapons were too good to pass up and by 1970 the PFLOAG not only reigned over the DLF but they controlled the Jebal.[66]

Considering many Bayt Kathir men and other Jebalis were part of the Dhofar Force (DF), a small security force belonging to the Sultan, it was not a huge surprise when there was an insurrection within the DF. In April 1966 when inspecting the DF at Razat, outside of Salalah, the Sultan came under attack by men in the force. In the end the Northern Front Regiment (NFR) under command of Lieutenant Colonel Sanders put down the revolt. Thirteen Jebali members escaped while thirty more were arrested. The failed attempt showed the danger of an insurgency since it was also discovered that dissidents were within the ranks since as early as 1962. However, the failed attack had little influence over the people of Salalah or the Sultan who after firing the DF commander, continued to maintain the DF after the attack.[67]

In the beginning the *adoo*, Omani word for enemy, were dependent on the population for their support and security.[68] Even after the PFLOAG started supporting the Jebalis with superior weapons, the rebel fighters still depended upon the population for security. The overall strategy was to infiltrate into northern Oman as well as Dhofar. Insurgent forces attacked SAF barracks as far north as Bid Bid and Izki. Even beyond

72

the Dhofar Force's infiltration and attempt on the Sultan's life, insurgents infiltrated the Sultan's Armed Forces. As late as 1973 several agents were uncovered serving as soldiers in the SAF. They were all executed by firing squad shortly afterward.[69]

DLF's and later PFLOAG's more immediate objective was subversion or outright capture of the town of Salalah–the capital of Dhofar.[70] The rebels would come in off the mountains and terrorize and intimidate the population. They would use torture, burning people and throwing them off the cliffs in order to gain their fear and obedience. If community leaders did not assent to their ways, they were assassinated and their children would then be abducted to Yemen for indoctrination.[71]

The *adoo* did not have the forces to meet head to head with the Sultan's Forces, so they conducted a war of attrition. Through mortar attacks, car bombs, mines along the road and ambushes in the Jebal against His Majesty's Forces the insurgents attempted to wear down the will and capabilities of the Omani Forces. The insurgents endeavored to erode the people's will to support a perceived illegitimate government by showing that they could not protect and defend the People of Oman. The ultimate goal was to overthrow or assassinate the Sultan and set up another form of government. In order to achieve the fear amongst the Dhofaris and to break the Omani soldiers' will to fight the rebels would torture and kill any of their captures. Unlike in Vietnam where some captives might end up in prisoner of war camps no such expectation existed in Oman. The *adoo* were so brutal that the standard operating procedure for the Sultan's forces, if unable to immediately extract downed pilots, was to bomb the wreckage to ensure that no living pilots fell into the hands of the enemy.[72]

73

The insurgents' strongholds were along the western border and interior of the country, up in the Jebal. The high altitude, numerous caves and deep wadis gave the *adoo* the perfect place to infiltrate, store caches, hide and defend. From the Jebal the *adoo* could pick the place and time to conduct attacks toward the cities along the Omani coast. The *adoo* still had to be supplied and they were unwilling or unable to conduct resupply on the Arabian Sea. Most of the resupply came from the People's Democratic Republic of Yemen. The insurgents brought in heavy weapons along these supply lines during the summer months when cloud cover over the Jebal precluded British forces from conducting airstrikes. Then in the dry winter months when SAF fighter bombers could dominate the battlespace, such weapons and material was hidden in the numerous caves that littered the area.[73] Initially the supplies came on the backs of camels through the Wadi Adawnib, but after the creation of the Hornbeam Line, a defensive obstacle barrier made up of wire and mines with over watching battle positions, supplies had to be brought in by individual insurgents carrying smaller loads (see Figure 9. Western Dhofar depicting the Defensive Belts Across the Jebal, page 93). This greatly reduced the amount of supplies and therefore bullets that the enemy could fire on the SAF and the number of mortar and artillery rounds that could be lobbed at the people in the local cities.[74]

Besides lobbing constant mortar and artillery fire on the Omani positions at Sarfait, the adoo also attempted more dramatic attacks to delegitimize the Sultan's government. In their continued attempts to show the locals that the government could not protect them, rebels planned a significant assault on the town of Mirbat. About 300 insurgents attempted to sneak into the area defended by a platoon sized element of Omani and eight British Special Air Service soldiers. In a preceding attack near the town several Omani soldiers escaped and warned Mirbat about the impending attack. Although outnumbered ten to one, the defenders of Mirbat beat back the insurgent attack with one British 25 pound artillery piece that they fired in direct fire mode and several close air support missions conducted by Strikemaster air to ground fighters. Also a squadron of British SAS that was due to rotate into the theater just happened to be on a firing range not too far from Mirbat and was able to arrive at the last minute and counterattack against the adoo. Estimates of enemy casualties ranged from sixty to two hundred. The failed attack ended up backfiring on the enemy and showed that the Sultan's Army could and would protect the Dhofari people.[75]

Sultan's Forces and Strategy

The Sultan's forces at the beginning of the 20th century ranged from 50 or 60 armed men defending the Sultan against initial attacks to a rather large robust military that included armored cars, engineers, a navy and a modern air force by 1975. This force increased dramatically after the Sultan Qaboos took over in 1970.[76] To lead such an expanded and modern force, the Sultan enlisted the help of the British.

76

The overall commander of His Majesty's Forces was a British general. During the fighting, Brigadier General John Graham and Major General Tim Creasey, who held this position, maintained a close advisory role with the Sultan.[77] There were four Omani infantry battalions within the SAF.[78] The main fighting force of the Omani land forces in Dhofar consisted of two Omani infantry battalions and two Baluchi infantry battalions supported by the Oman artillery and an armored car squadron.[79] Two were deployed to the war zone in Dhofar at a time while the other two were sent north to re-fit, re-arm, recover and re-train. These rotations varied depending on the ongoing missions, but they were roughly nine to ten months in length.[80] The commander of Dhofar Brigade, which was always a British officer, commanded all of the Sultan's Forces to include naval and air assets while they were deployed to the war zone.[81] Eventually, as other countries allied with the Sultan, this force developed into an international force made up of Baluchis, Indians, Pakistanis, Iranians, Jordanians, Egyptians and British as well as Omanis and consisted of approximately 10,000 men.[82] The Dhofar Brigade commander, who also held a seat on the Dhofar Development Committee, vetted all of his campaigns and large military operations through the committee which was chaired by the Dhofar Wali or provincial governor, every Sunday morning.

Each infantry battalion consisted of transportation, signal, reconnaissance, mortar, engineer and animal transport platoons within the headquarters company and three rifle companies of four platoons each. The Baluch Guard battalions were less well equipped and performed the static guard duty in platoon to company size elements freeing up the Omani infantry to conduct the offensive operations. The Oman artillery consisted of several 25 pounder and 75mm guns as well as one 5.5 inch howitzer. This indirect fire asset was split into three elements: one for support of the RAF at Salalah, one Western

Approach Troop and one air mobile element for offensive operations. The Sultan's Navy

consisted of one motorized dhow and the Royal yacht, *Al Sa'id*. The SOAF consisted of

a strike squadron made up of Provost Strikemasters, a helicopter squadron made up of

two reconnaissance helicopters and six troop Agusta Bell 205's which could carry up to

12 troops or one ton of supplies at a time, and one Air Support Squadron which included

one Caribou and three Skyvan aircraft. Great efforts had to be made to clear runways on

the Jebal before any of the fixed wing aircraft from the support squadron could land on

them, so the real workhorse of the war was the Bell helicopter. Rounding off the Sultan's

forces were eleven *Firqats* (Arabic word for unit), which were recruited volunteer units

or militia usually made up of surrendered guerillas. These *Firqats* ranged from platoon

to company size strength.[83] Near the end of the war the Shah of Iran sent large amounts

of conventional forces over to help out the Sultan. Iranian brigade sized elements fought,

although not very impressively, near the end of the war on the western Dhofar Jebal, west

of what was the Hornbeam Line and near what would eventually be called the Damavand

Line.[84] At the conclusion of the war in 1975, the British ground contingent of the Dhofar

Brigade was renamed the British Army Element Dhofar (BAED), presumably to signify a

change in the makeup of the Sultan's Force as more Omani officers began to take

leadership positions.[85]

Theorizing Small Wars

Although the British small war doctrine had not yet been written, there were

three, possibly four, academic works that had been completed during and prior to the

conclusion of the Dhofar Insurgency that were influential in how the Sultan, closely advised by his British dignitaries and military officers, fought the war. Robert

Thompson, Julian Paget and Frank Kitson, all British subjects who wrote books dealing

with counterinsurgency, used prior experiences in the multiple guerilla wars leading up to

Oman.[86] Additionally, Lieutenant Colonel John McCuen, a serving United States Army

officer, wrote *The Art of Counter-Revolutionary War: The Strategy of Counter-*

insurgency, which was also printed in Great Britain.[87] It appears at least some, if not all,

of these men collaborated on their ideas.

Lieutenant Colonel McCuen, in response to mounting casualties in Vietnam, was

grappling with an effective way to approach what was not new, but certainly alien to

American forces fighting in South East Asia. He claimed that previous works had

discussed aspects of revolutionary wars, but none, except that of America's enemies, was

all encompassing. The Army officer stated he was attempting to fill the void by

developing a set of guiding principles that stressed ―political, psychological, and military

fundamentals" in order to ―conduct this new type of warfare."[88]

He clearly delineated the importance of securing the population, but argued that

the civilian population must be able to self-defend against insurgent organizations.[89] His

main strategy, the oil spot strategy which he recommended to defeat an insurgency, was

based on French General Boyer de Latour's approach to solving the Indochina insurgency

between 1945 to 1954. Lack of support from the French government and lack of troops

to secure the cleared areas eventually led to General de Latour's failure to defeat the

insurgency. McCuen, however, argued that the clearing, building and expanding of

friendly bases, until the bases encompassed all of South Vietnam, would eventually

work.[90] He also called for small units to conduct territorial offensive ―nomadic" action against the enemy within designated areas. These small forces would not base anywhere within the area, but instead would constantly move throughout the area to raid, attack and ambush guerilla forces.[91] The focus on these forces was to be small, fast and flexible so that they could be nimble enough to catch the elusive guerilla forces.[92] McCuen, based on the French model of the Special Administrative Sections (French SAS--not to be confused with the British SAS), and Urban Administrative Sections (SAU) used in Algeria, called for the development of Military Civic Action Teams. Their primary focus was on reorganizing local populations to neutralize the insurgent's indoctrination of the local villages.[93]

Similar to British attempts at moving populations in Malaya and the French in Algeria, McCuen argued for consolidation of several smaller villages into bigger ones to better defend the population against insurgents.[94] Lieutenant Colonel McCuen's plan also called for constant vigilance in attacking into non-base areas, ground not controlled by friendly forces, with significant ground forces. In order to make these strikes into the interior, McCuen called for ―Forbidden Zones." Anybody within that zone was considered enemy.[95] Lastly, McCuen mentioned the use of counter-guerilla teams to train, equip and lead local bands of forces.[96]

At the same time McCuen published his work on counterinsurgency, Sir Robert Thompson published the tenth work in an International Security Studies Series. His book was developed from his experiences in Malaya from 1948 to 1960 and in South Vietnam from 1961 through 1965.[97] Thompson focused on how the insurgency was developed and executed in those two countries. Thompson explained that due to the history of Japanese rule over the Chinese and the need to adopt a similar ―legitimate, progressive and desirable" cause, the Chinese Communists adopted the cause of anti-colonialism or in the later case of the United States, anti-imperialism.[98] Thompson pointed out that the platforms were generic and, at least in the open, purported very lofty and progressive goals. They targeted all levels of society, but were directed more so to the youth. After gaining many arms and supplies, the insurgents switched from spouting such lofty ideals to a more coercive approach along the lines of Mao Tse-Tung's philosophy that ―political power grows out of the barrel of a gun."[99]

Leaders at all levels that did not yield to the insurgency were summarily discredited and then murdered. Along with murdering central political figures, any other local civilians that helped the British, French or eventually the American cause, earned retaliation from the insurgents. Additionally, they attacked communication infrastructure, police stations, small military outposts and other government agencies in an attempt to cause panic within the population and to delegitimize the government's ability to provide common services. Slowly the s gained control of the populations until they were in sufficient strength to attack larger military formations. The whole time they were constantly recruiting more locals to join their ranks.[100] Despite heavy losses the s were able to continue their campaigns due to their very successful recruitment efforts. Despite the effectiveness of the Vietnam insurgency, Thompson showed that only about one percent of the population actively supported or took part in insurgent activity.[101]

Thompson then prescribed the five basic principles that needed to be followed to defeat such a threat. First and foremost, Thompson stated that ―an insurgent movement is a war for the people."[102] In order to win over those people, Thompson argued that the government of the country must have a very organized and effective administrative

81

structure. Without such an apparatus all the well intentioned projects designed to win over the populace will be for naught. The government's aim must be to –establish and maintain a free, independent and united country."[103]

Sir Robert proposed that –the government must function in accordance with law."[104] He made a compelling case that discounted the argument that you should fight as savagely as your enemy and ignore your own laws based off your society's values and morals.[105] Thompson argued that such tactics create more problems than they solve and eventually will cause the government to lose legitimacy for not fulfilling –its contractual obligation to the people."[106]

Thompson's third principle stated that there must be an overarching plan that covered both political and security as well as social and economic measures. The government must prioritize not only how, but also where, it spends its limited resources. Sir Thompson explained that even if security operations are effective, if such operations are not followed up by positive civil measures in the realm of governance, education, infrastructure and business investment eventually the civilian population will lose faith in the government. The government plan needed to be focused in enough detail to give a vision toward accomplishing the overall goals, but flexible enough to react to unexpected successes and failures.

The plan must be focused on defeating the political subversion and not primarily focused on defeating the guerillas. Thompson gave the analogy of removing the –little fishes" from –the water;" the little fishes being the guerillas, and the water being the people. As long as the government subversion continued, the insurgents would have a base from which to gather supplies, move freely amongst and gain recruits from the populace.[107] This in effect is backward-engineering of one of Mao's main principles spouted in his *Little Red Book*, which stated that the revolutionary garners his support from the people. In order to accomplish this, Thompson spoke of the three objects for creating "strategic hamlets" in Vietnam. The three objects were to protect the population, unite the people positively on the side of the government and to create areas of social, economic and political development.[108] Thompson, however, failed in understanding the Vietnamese's connection with the land and moving villages into strategic hamlets failed miserably. It is clear to see he understood the insurgent center of gravity, but failed in his strategy of how to attack that center of gravity.

The British theorist finished up his list of principles by stating the need to first secure the developed regions where security and prosperity already existed. Starting in these regions was naturally easier since there was less subversion and dissident activity, and maintaining security in these areas would give the government forces an early victory which in turn would build some confidence within the security forces. Some outer regions might fall into insurgent hands with this methodology, but Thompson argued going after the insurgents in those outer regions without the ability to sustain the security would ultimately lead to losing ground to the insurgency, which would give the momentum to the insurgents.[109]

Although not one of his five principles, Thompson's most enlightening comment about the Malayan and Vietnamese insurgencies dealt with size and makeup of the security apparatus. Thompson stated that the centralized and conventional structure of Vietnamese forces was designed to defend against an invading army and not to fight a counterinsurgency, which contradicted the American perspective that a conventional soldier could defeat an insurgent. On the other hand, a British general in Malaya when asked what his role was, stated ―as far as I can see, the only thing a divisional commander has to do in this sort of war is to go [a]round seeing that the troops have got their beer!"[110] A counterinsurgency fight is fought at the lowest levels: squads, platoons and companies. The construction of a big army, however, causes these squad, platoon and company leaders to be responsive to colonels and generals, and therefore ignoring the desires of local leaders. These generals do not know what is happening in a province, village or hamlet like that local leader does and therefore are not in the best position to fight that war.

Big conventional armies conduct conventional maneuvers against other big conventional armies. Such maneuvers do not defeat insurgents and most likely cause more insurgents. In worst case scenarios these maneuvers cause collateral damage including friendly deaths and, at a minimum, such large actions disrupt the daily lives of the local inhabitants. Not only will such armies be ineffective against the insurgency, but they will also cause the significant power to sit with the army leaders instead of the civilian leadership, attempting to gain legitimacy. Instead of worrying about governing the people during precarious times, the political leader ends up devoting time and energy to maintaining control of such an army. Also, such big armies draw talent away from government positions and less high-qualified people end up taking posts in critical positions within the fledgling government. A big army is not only unwieldy; its ranks are often crowded with undisciplined soldiers who harass the population in the outer areas creating more ill will toward the government, making civilian aid projects in such regions ineffective.[111] Though no definitive evidence exists, it seems the Sultan's strategy follows the principles of Sir Thompson's advocacy.

British Army Lieutenant Colonel Julian Paget wrote a piece that was published in 1967. Drawing on operations in Malaya, Kenya and Cyprus, the British officer's primary thesis was that counter-insurgencies were conducted in three phases. Phase one happened when there was a swell in violence and lawlessness with a portion of the population that was against the government. In phase two, the government is essentially on the defensive and the insurgents have the initiative. During phase three, the government seizes the initiative and puts pressure on the insurgents ending either in military defeat or a political solution.[112]

Paget stated that the first priority of planning should be toward the government and the establishment of a clear political strategy that a viable long-term military strategy could facilitate. Along with this aim there were five "essentials" for conducting counterinsurgency operations.[113] Firstly, in what Paget terms "civil-military understanding," he stressed that the military must realize that the war will be won by civilian leadership supported by a joint military campaign. His second essential of "command and control," is analogous to the principle of Unity of Command. Paget explains that although a civilian leader needs to be the ultimate "Director of Operations," he needs to have a joint staff of both military and police security forces.[114] Paget also asserted the importance of integrated intelligence during all phases of the insurgency, and although he stated that it was not essential, support of the populace in intelligence gathering was a great battlefield multiplier. Lieutenant Colonel Paget declared the importance of greater counterinsurgent mobility through the use of active patrolling and air mobility in order to quickly move to the insurgent activity. Lastly, the British Army officer stated that men fighting a counterinsurgency will be fighting in small units, and in physical isolation for long periods of time. They must have the highest initiative and particular skill sets required for an unconventional fight, as well as the adeptness to deal with government organizations at the lowest levels in order to defeat the insurgents. In order to have troops that can conduct this type of warfare, considerable effort must be put into training these men in not only what the enemy looks and fights like, but what the local government and security forces look like.[115] Another British officer, based off his experiences, reinforced and expanded Sir Robert's and Paget's assertions.

Although not early enough to affect the opening of Dhofar insurgency, British Brigadier Frank Kitson published a piece in 1971 that might have been the genesis of American Army doctrine in the future. He, like Paget, used his experiences in Cyprus, Malaya and Kenya to form his understanding of counterinsurgent warfare. Any question of its importance in American and British military thought is answered by a glowing preface written by Lieutenant General Richard G. Stillwell and a resounding foreword penned by General Sir Michael Carver. At the time of Kitson's publication, Stillwell was the Deputy Chief of Staff for Military Operations of the United States Army and General Carver was the British Chief of the General Staff.[116]

Brigadier Kitson, after explaining the nuances to describe the current irregular fight, settled on subversion and insurgency for his primary efforts in describing the enemy forces.[117] Similar to Paget, Kitson described in some detail the phases of an insurgency as well as the importance of integrating military, police and civil support operations into one coherent workable plan. Also similar to Paget and Thompson, Kitson reiterated the importance of a highly trained force, but goes further to identify the need

for the counterinsurgent force having additional skills of psychological operations, civil

affairs and unconventional warfare.[118] His most influential chapter seems to have been

his analysis of what he terms "the handling of information" which describes in some

detail the intelligence collection techniques practiced to gather information on the

insurgent forces.[119]

Kitson, not dissimilar to both Paget and Thompson, aptly argued that since the

hardest effort in an insurgency is finding the enemy insurgents and those who support

them, then intelligence is critical to defeating an insurgency. He described one of the

most painful processes within intelligence efforts toward a counterinsurgency is the fact

that often the information is out of date before soldiers can conduct direct action against

an insurgent.[120] Kitson stated that intelligence organizations are responsible for

providing background information on the enemy and can be helpful in developing such

information, but it is the operational commander that is ultimately responsible for

developing that information into something his soldiers can act upon.

Based on experiences from Malaya, Kitson offered a scenario of a way to fight a

communist insurgency in a wooded, sparsely populated area that he stated could be

anywhere from Norway to Malaya. Small units led by the best leaders move into the

villages spending lots of time with the inhabitants to build, although he does not define it

as such, what we know as situational awareness. Over time the leaders conduct surveys

of the population and, after building up situational understanding, they begin to deduce

through analysis where the insurgents are located. Only after they build up enough

intelligence to take out the networks do they arrest the leaders. Constant presence in the village is necessary to protect the villagers and over time to win over their allegiance. The force must be disciplined and take measures for securing themselves, while not alienating the populace. Although there are setbacks, eventually the tide turns toward the government forces and information starts to come in faster and more accurate and most of the communist insurgency threat is reduced to a point where home guard forces can provide their own security. The government forces are now ready to push on to another area to conduct the same mission over again until the insurgency is defeated within the entire country. Of primary importance to Kitson's example was that logical, but gifted analysis of very rudimentary and fragmented intelligence reports by the best leaders controlling a small disciplined forced over a very long period of constant presence is what defeats an insurgency.[121]

As in most cases, insurgent forces maintained the initiative, growing in size, amount of support and scope of operations in the early years of the war because government military forces were slow to react and the Sultan made no effort at appeasement or reconciliation. The SAF, augmented by air and artillery assets, usually defeated the enemy when it found them. However, as Americans were finding out in Vietnam, focusing on killing the enemy did not attack the center of gravity: the population. For every insurgent killed, more regional fighters were infiltrating into Oman and support for the insurgency was gaining ground. It was not until luck, fate or maybe even a little push from agents of the empire that fortunes began to change for the Sultan and his allies.

As America learned in both Korea and Vietnam, finding the right person to lead a new government in a foreign country is one of the most challenging endeavors.

However, the British government had a trump card up their sleeve in the form of Qaboos bin Sa'id Al Sa'id, Crown Prince of Oman. Sultan Qaboos, the 14th successor in his family's rule of Muscat and Oman was, after all, educated at Sandhurst, the British Royal Military Academy in 1960. Qaboos spent an additional year with the Scottish Rifles in Western Germany and two additional years studying local government in England before returning to Oman in 1964. Despite his father imposing house arrest on young Qaboos after his return, he was well aware of his country's perilous position and all too cognizant of his father's inaction. As the situation in Oman got worse with attacks in northern Oman against the Sultan's military installations, Qaboos, at the age of thirty, overthrew his father in an almost bloodless coup, sending the old Sultan to a comfortable exile in England in July of 1970.[122] Some have postulated that the coup was inspired by British agents within Oman.[123] Regardless of how or why the events transpired, with the young Sultan's ascendency, Britain now had, in the eyes of the Dhofaris, a legitimate ruler who understood the need for advancing technologies and freedoms of the people of Oman. This was the tipping point in the war.

The Sultan established a committee to run the war in Dhofar. The Dhofar Development Committee, chaired by Sheik Braik bin Hamoud, a chief conspirator in dethroning the old Sultan, spent 218 million British Pounds in Dhofar to rebuild the infrastructure while simultaneously running the war.[124] The committee's strategy to defeat the insurgency was simple and not far reaching. They understood their culture and understood that by bringing prosperity to the region they could defeat the communist threat. In fact the focus of the Sultan's Armed Forces was not to destroy, kill or capture the *adoo*, but —to scure Dhofar for civilian development."[125] As Ian Gardiner puts it;

89

—those six words . . . unambiguous, crisp and entirely to the point . . . gave an endstate . . . and overall purpose" to the Sultan's Forces.[126] After success with the projects within the communities in Dhofar, there was little doubt to the *adoo* that they were no longer welcome. Their choices were limited to leaving the town or village and heading into Yemen or joining the Sultan's forces as *firqat*.[127] To help along with this effort, Sultan Qaboos shortly after assuming the Sultanate released some prisoners and offered a general amnesty period to Omani rebels to denounce the rebellion and join the SAF as *firqat*. Many original DLF members, sickened by the atheist s, when offered this period chose to surrender. [128]

The *firqat* in many cases were Jebali tribesmen who had fought on the side of the insurgency and then switched to the side of the Sultan. There were several reasons for them switching sides and, without trivializing it too much, in many cases they came for the rials, Omani money, offered by the Sultan for weapons and mines. Also the ideology forced upon them by their Chinese and Russian handlers was not their own. One of the

greatest reasons the Jebalis joined the side of the Sultan was that he had won ―their hearts

and minds" by changing the ways of his father and therefore taking away the reasons for

them to rebel against the government of Oman in the first place. Lastly, according to Ian

Gardiner, they joined because they wanted to be on the winning side. Although they

were hard to train, unreliable in fights, untrustworthy since many of their relatives still

fought with the enemy, they were critical to the success of the war because their

participation gave the force legitimacy. Once they joined the fight, it could no longer be

said that it was an army of occupation. It was now locals fighting for their land. They

were critical for intelligence gathering and were perfect for reconnaissance. Since they

grew up where they were fighting, their knowledge of the land was undeniable and in

great demand by the Sultan's forces. With every Jebali fighting on the side of the Sultan,

that was one less enemy that they were fighting against.[129]

After winning the initial moral victory, the government forces established

permanent defenses in the central and eastern Jebal. These defensive positions, along

with active patrolling and ambushing, had limited the *adoo's* freedom of movement.

Once the *adoo* was clear from an area, the army would secure it so they could not come

back into the area. As per the mission statement of the Dhofar Development Committee

which stated the main purpose of the military action was ―to secure Dhofar for civilian

development," public works projects began in these secured areas. Led by the Civil Aid

Department, schools and clinics were built, wells drilled and Mosques erected. They also

worked on farm projects and built roads.[130] After securing the populations within the

towns, Oman's forces focused on isolating the *adoo* in the center and west of Dhofar.

The initial attempt at isolating the *adoo* was in the form of the Leopard Line of 1971, but this line had failed for lack of an effective barrier obstacle.[131] The later establishment of the Hornbeam Line effectively isolated the *adoo* in accordance with the overall strategy.

Failing to garner any more support from the locals, FPLOAG rebels had to receive almost all of their support from across the border in Yemen. To combat this the SAF had to establish defensive positions along the wadis to the west of Dhofar. In order to interdict these supply lines, an Omani infantry battalion was placed in Sarfait. From this position the SAF could attack and cut the *adoo's* supply lines. However, Sarfait was much too high at approximately three thousand feet above sea level, compared to the actual infiltration routes which ran about a thousand feet above sea level. The battalion could not effectively interdict the lines so it was initially fairly useless, but to pull the battalion would have been admitting some failure, so instead the battalion stayed in Sarfait.[132]

After the failed attempt at the Leopard Line of 1971, the Hornbeam Line was established which ran far enough west into the Jebal that any persons found in the area could be assumed as enemy. Unlike the Leopard Line of 1971, the Hornbeam Line was made up of platoon and company size positions that covered the entire width of the infiltration routes from Yemen. Vast amounts of wire, and mines were strung along this line and constant patroling and ambushes by the SAF along this line strangled the lines of communication for the rebel forces to supply or reinforce the PFLOAG elements within Dhofar (see Figure 9. Western Dhofar depicting the Defensive Belts Across the Jebal, page 93).[133]

By placing the Hornbeam Line in place on the Jebal west of the population's center, the military outpost would interdict the supply and reinforcement elements coming in from the People's Democratic Republic of Yemen (PDRY) and it also kept the *adoo* busy attacking the outposts instead of focusing on the civilian populations in Dhofar. From these positions British and Omani forces set up ambushes on the infiltrating *adoo*. [134] The Sultan decreed that any armed men in groups of three or more outside the perimeter of a settlement were to be considered rebels.[135] *Firqat*, that had switched sides, also helped identify caches, infiltration routes and, with the use of the SOAF and SAF ground forces, rebel elements attempting to fight their way through the Jebal into Dhofar were destroyed.

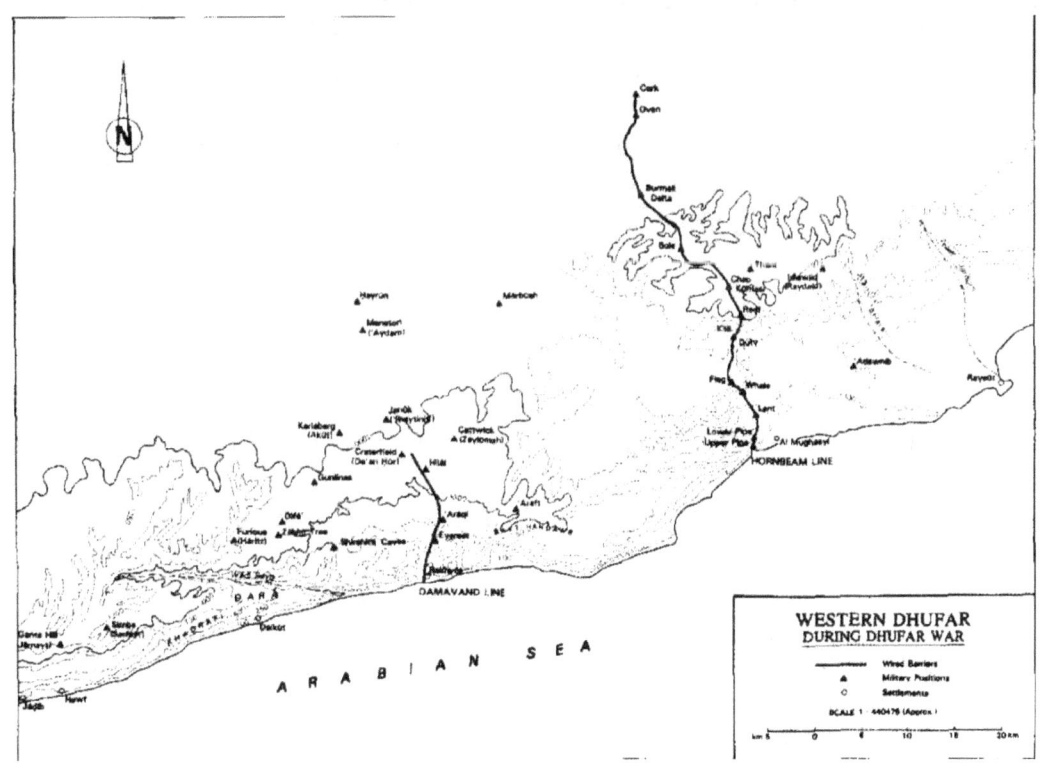

Figure 9.   Western Dhofar depicting the Defensive belts across the Jebal
Source: J. E. Peterson, *Oman's Insurgencies: The Sultanate's Struggle for Supremacy*, (London: SAQI, 2007), 493. Note: Exact position of the Leopard Line could not be established, but it is assumed that it was east of the Hornbeam Line.

In 1975 the Sultan declared victory against the communist insurgents. Although sporadic incidents would continue to crop up over the next several years, the Sultan's forces were in position to defeat any significant attempts at subversion, dissidence and open rebellion. In the grand scheme of the Cold War, Oman was just a blip on the screen. Despite the country's strategic location and the duration of the Dhofar insurgency, the conflict did not even register in *War in Peace*, a book which listed every conflict from the rise of Mao Tse Tung in China to the Iran-Iraq War in 1980. Although having sections on Cuba and international terrorism and urban guerillas in South America, this far reaching account of warfare since the end of World War II did not even list Oman within the index.[136] In the end the war was won not by military campaigns against the communist insurgents, but by a multitude of other factors.

In fact, the lack of emphasis on the country might have been one of the more important factors why the British and their Omani counterparts were able to defeat the insurgent forces threatening the Sultanate. Instead of large conventional forces that will invariably have disciplinary issues and could leave a potentially large, negative footprint on the country, the expert force that the British did deploy to fight for the Sultan were elite volunteers that were vetted both in England and Oman. Because of their makeup these soldiers were able to adapt quickly to the cultural and religious intricacies of the country, thereby being better able to lead the Omani forces while not offending the local populous. This small force was not under the leadership of a high ranking British general in Muscat, but rather the Dhofar Development Committee which was made up of the civilian leadership from the region and chaired by the Governor of Dhofar. This allowed for highly effective synchronized civil military relations that in the end were the right combination to provide the security and establish the government infrastructure that would prove the Sultan's commitment to his subjects.

Ultimately the Sultan himself had the most decisive effect on the winning of the war. Diplomatically, Sultan Qaboos worked with regional countries to receive additional forces to help combat the communist invaders. This freed up his own forces to conduct more direct action against the enemy while also partially showing legitimacy of his new government. He also offered a period of amnesty that reconciled many of the disenfranchised DLF members back into his kingdom. Informationally, the Sultan and the SAS used an information campaign built to propagate the new strengths of the Sultan's initiatives to fix the elements of his father's regime that disenfranchised the large number of initial insurgent forces. Economically the Sultan focused a majority of his national budget to not only fund the military force he needed to secure his Dhofar Region, but also to develop the area with industry, communication and other infrastructure. This, along with the military's ability to secure the citizens in the region and the large number of Jebalis that left the insurgency and came to the side of the Sultan, added to the legitimacy that eventually won over the populous in effect strangling the insurgency of both personnel and support from within the country.

---

[1]Thomas P.M. Barnett, *The Pentagon's New Map: War and Peace in the Twenty-First Century* (New York: G. P. Putnam's Sons 2004).

95

[2]*Persian Gulf States* (Washington, D.C., 1994)., 257, 274; J. E. Peterson, *Oman's Insurgencies: The Sultanate's Struggles for Supremacy,* (London, 2007), 59.

[3]John Akehurst, *We Won a War: The Campaign in Oman 1965-1975,* (Southampton: 1982), 12-15.

[4]Peterson, *Oman's Insurgencies: The Sultanate's Struggles for Supremacy,* 47, 51, 61.

[5]Akehurst, *We Won a War: The Campaign in Oman 1965-1975,* 11-13.

[6]Ibid., 259-263, 304. Official estimates put the size of the country at 300,000 kilometers, but most foreign observers claim 212,000 kilometers which is roughly the size of the state of Kansas. Today in Oman there are approximately two million people in the country with almost a quarter of the country being comprised of foreigners.

[7]J. E. Peterson, *Oman's Insurgencies: The Sultanate's Struggles for Supremacy,* (London: 2007), 32; *Persian Gulf States,* 261; *Persian Gulf States* (Washington, DC: 1994), 259-263; Ian Gardiner, *In the Service of the Sultan: A First Hand Account of the Dhofar Insurgency,* (South Yorkshire, England: 2007), 37-38. Falaj, translated in Arabic, means distribution.

[8]Sultanate of Oman, www.omanet.om/english, (2009). Official Sultanate of Oman Information website.

[9]Alexander Melamid, —Dhofar," *Geographical Review,* 74 no. 1 (1984), 106-9, 107.

[10]Melamid, —Dhofar", 106-108.

[11]There are many similarities to the difficulties the British SAS and the Firqats had in the Jebal to what American soldiers face in the Korengal Valley fighting the Taliban.

[12]Ian Gardiner, *In the Service of the Sultan: A First Hand Account of the Dhofar Insurgency* (South Yorkshire, England: 2007), 32.

[13]John Akehurst, *We Won a War: The Campaign in Oman 1965-1975,* (Southampton: 1982), 4, 9, 11.

[14]Tony Jeapes, *SAS: Operation Oman* (Nashville, TN: 1980), 47.

[15]Niccolo Machiavelli, *The Prince,* (Fort Wayne; IN: 2006), 29.

[16]Gardiner, *Service of the Sultan,* 34.

[17]Ibid.,40; Akehurst, *We Won a War: The Campaign in Oman 1965-1975,* 12.

[18] Gardiner, *Service of the Sultan*, 40-41.

[19] Gardiner, *Service of the Sultan*, 57.

[20] Jeapes, *Operation Oman*, 51.

[21] Peterson, *Oman's Insurgencies: The Sultanate's Struggles for Supremacy*, 107-108.

[22] Valerie J. Hoffman, ─Ibadi Islam: An Introduction," (2009).

[23] Ibid.

[24] *Persian Gulf States*, 19, 264.

[25] Ibid., xxvi.

[26] Ibid.,1, *Persian Gulf States*, 22-23.

[27] Peterson, *Oman's Insurgencies: The Sultanate's Struggles for Supremacy*, 41-46.

[28] Tony Jeapes, *SAS: Operation Oman*, (Nashville, TN: 1980), 28.

[29] Gardiner, *Service of the Sultan*, 57, 58.

[30] Ibid., 11.

[31] *Persian Gulf States*, 336.

[32] Robert Thompson, ed., *War in Peace: Conventional and Guerilla Warfare Since 1945* (New York: 1981), v-viii.

[33] Thompson, *Defeating Communist Insurgency: The Lessons of Malaya and Vietnam*, 169.

[34] The word men, instead of soldiers, was purposely used since, especially in the early days, most of the men fighting for the Sultan did not have any formal training.

[35] Akehurst, *We Won a War: The Campaign in Oman 1965-1975*, 1, 31; Peterson, *Oman's Insurgencies: The Sultanate's Struggles for Supremacy*,36, 41, 103. Quote is on p. 103.

[36] Jeapes, *Operation Oman*, 29-30.

[37] Peterson, *Oman's Insurgencies: The Sultanate's Struggles for Supremacy*, 150.

[38] Akehurst, *We Won a War: The Campaign in Oman 1965-1975*, 31-32.

[39]Peterson, *Oman's Insurgencies: The Sultanate's Struggles for Supremacy*, 20, 116, 150, 291-292. Later the Sultan of Oman's Air Force (SOAF) was re-labeled the Royal Air Force of Oman (RAFO).

[40]Jeapes, *Operation Oman*, 11, 15.

[41]When discussing British advisors, it could mean either British officers on loan to the Sultan, seconded officers, retired officers or British SAS. They all advised and led Omani forces.

[42]Ibid., 29-32.

[43]Ibid., 29-30.

[44]Ibid., 35.

[45]Ibid., 45.

[46]Ibid., 44.

[47]Ibid., 42-43.

[48] Ibid., 44.

[49]Ibid., 100.

[50]Akehurst, *We Won a War: The Campaign in Oman 1965-1975*, 2.

[51]Ibid., 30.

[52]Ibid., 33-34.

[53]Ibid., 48-49.

[54]Ibid., 154.

[55]Ibid., 39.

[56]Ibid., 40-41.

[57]Jeapes, *Operation Oman*, 31.

[58]Akehurst, *We Won a War: The Campaign in Oman 1965-1975*, 12-15.

[59]Jeapes, *Operation Oman*, 24.

[60]Peterson, *Oman's Insurgencies: The Sultanate's Struggles for Supremacy*, 186-187. The following were some of the opposition groups in Oman: Arab Nationalists'

Movement (ANM), Dhofari's who lived in Cairo, Kuwait and Iraq; Dhofar Benevolent Society (DBS) initially created as a true benevolent group, the DBS became a front for the ANM; Dhofar Soldier's Organization (DSO), disaffected soldiers from what is not the area of the U.A.E who recruited Dhofar soldiers in Qatar, Hizb al-Zahf (Party of Advance), some doubt whether this was an actual party or just in the minds of the Dhofari soldiers; al-Kaff al-Aswad (The Black Palm) Initially based in Salalah and made up of khuddam, the group broke up when the DLF came about; Dhofar Liberation Front, probably initially inspired by Musallim of the Kathir tribe.

[61]Ibid., 188-189. Musallim held several jobs but failed to show up for duty as a soldier and was also fired as a generator mechanic. Initially arrested he was released when the tribe promised better behavior from him.

[62]Jeapes, *Operation Oman,* 24-25.

[63]Ibid., 1-2.

[64]Ibid., 195-197.

[65]Stephen F. Howe, ―Fighting the Global War on Terro Tolerably: Augmenting the Global Counter Insurgency Strategy with Surrogates" (Monograph, School of Advanced Military Studies, Fort Leavenworth, KS, 2007), 27.

[66]Jeapes, *Operation Oman,* 25.

[67]Peterson, *Oman's Insurgencies: The Sultanate's Struggles for Supremacy,* 202-203.

[68]Ibid., 74.

[69]Ibid., 74.

[70]Ibid., 72

[71]Ibid., 73.

[72]Ibid., 63.

[73]Melamid, ―Dhofar," 107.

[74]Ibid.,77-79.

[75]Ibid.,67-70.

[76]Akehurst, *We Won a War: The Campaign in Oman 1965-1975,* 31.

[77]Ibid., 53-54.

[78]Ian Gardiner stated that there were four regiments as opposed to battalions, but several other sources, including Akehurst, who commanded the Dhofar Brigade and Peterson list these units as battalions. To add to this confusion a British regiment can have anywhere between one and seventeen battalions in it. Gardiner, possibly may have been lumping the Baluchi battalions within his assessment to come up with the regimental formation, but given how the Baluchi battalions where fought, at platoon and company level, it would be misleading at best to define the units as regiments.

[79]Akehurst, *We Won a War: The Campaign in Oman 1965-1975*, 32-33.

[80]Ibid., 29.

[81]Akehurst, *We Won a War: The Campaign in Oman 1965-1975*, 32; Peterson, *Oman's Insurgencies: The Sultanate's Struggles for Supremacy*, 284-285.

[82]Ibid., 51, 52.

[83]Peterson, *Oman's Insurgencies: The Sultanate's Struggles for Supremacy*, 284-285.

[84]Ibid., 161.

[85]Ibid., 394.

[86]Ibid.

[87]John J. McCuen, *The Art of Counter-Revolutionary War: The Strategy of Counter-insurgency* (Harrisburg: 1966). Interestingly LTC McCuen inserted a note at the beginning of his work stating that "the opinions expressed are those of the author" and not of "the Department of the Army or Defense."

[88]Ibid., 19.

[89]Ibid., 107.

[90]Ibid., 196-199.

[91]A similar approach was chosen by British forces in southern Iraq during Operation Iraqi Freedom.

[92]Ibid., 206-208.

[93]Ibid., 225-229.

[94]Ibid., 231-232.

[95]Ibid., 236-238.

[96]Ibid., 239-240.

[97]Sir Robert Thompson, *Defeating Communist Insurgency: The Lessons of Malaya and Vietnam* (New York: 1966), 9.

[98]Ibid., 21.

[99]Ibid., 25- 27, quotation on 27.

[100]Ibid., 25-41.

[101]Ibid., 49.

[102]Ibid., 51.

[103]Ibid.

[104]Ibid., 52.

[105]Ralph Peters, *Fighting for the Future: Will America Triumph?,* (Mechanicsburg, PA: 1999), ix; Ralph Peters also made the argument more recently in an article in the American Legion's monthly magazine, *The Legion.*

[106]Thompson, *Defeating Communist Insurgency: The Lessons of Malaya and Vietnam*, 54.

[107]Ibid., 55.

[108]Ibid.,123-125.

[109]Ibid., 57-58.

[110]Ibid., 61.

[111]Ibid.,58-62.

[112]Julian Paget, *Counter-Insurgency Operations: Techniques of Guerilla Warfare* (New York: 1967), 7.

[113]Ibid., 158-159.

[114]Ibid., 159-160.

[115]Ibid., 165-167.

[116]Frank Kitson, *Low Intensity Operations: Subversion, Insurgency, Peace-keeping* (Harrisburg, PA: 1971), ix-xi.

[117]Ibid., 3-4.

[118]Ibid., ix-x, 77-79, 188-197.

[119]Ibid., 95-131.

[120]Advisory experiences in Iraq with the Iraqi National Police bear out Kitson's argument, especially if the police units are being advised by American military officers to approach each event with the typical 72 hour planning cycle that conventional forces use to plan military operations.

[121]Kitson, *Low Intensity Operations: Subversion, Insurgency, Peace-keeping*, 95-131.

[122]Peterson, *Oman's Insurgencies: The Sultanate's Struggles for Supremacy*, 31-32, 37; Akehurst, *We Won a War: The Campaign in Oman 1965-1975*, 16.

[123]Howe, ―Fighting the Global War on Terror Tolerably: Augmenting the Global Counter Insurgency Strategy with Surrogates,‖ 28. Originally cited in Peter Harclerode's *Fighting Dirty*, 413; Akehurst, *We Won a War: The Campaign in Oman 1965-1975*, 15. Akehurst who commanded the Dhofar Brigade, was somewhat cryptic in his description of the coup alluding to the fact that Qaboos might have had help from the British. Peterson, *Oman's Insurgencies: The Sultanate's Struggles for Supremacy*, 242-244. The old Sultan, after having been shot, surrendered to British officer Lieutenant Colonel Teddy Turnill who escorted the wounded ex-Sultan out of the palace and eventually on to England where he would live out the rest of his days.

[124]Ian F. W. Beckett, ―Insurgency in Iraq: An Historical Perspective,‖ (Carlisle, PA: 2005), 13.

[125]Ibid., 52.

[126]Ibid., 52.

[127]Ibid., 73-74.

[128]Jeapes, *Operation Oman*, 28.

[129]Ibid., 156-159.

[130]Gardiner, *Service of the Sultan*, 72-73.

[131]Ibid., Gardiner, *Service of the Sultan*, 75.

[132]Ibid., 65.

[133]Gardiner, *Service of the Sultan*, 55.

[134]Ibid., 79, 97.

[135]Peterson, *Oman's Insurgencies: The Sultanate's Struggles for Supremacy*, 207.

[136]Thompson, ed., *War in Peace: Conventional and Guerilla Warfare Since 1945*, v.

CHAPTER 4

ANALYSIS

Greece, Oman and Counterinsurgency Doctrine

> This conflict is a prolonged irregular campaign, a violent struggle for legitimacy and influence over the population. The use of force plays a role, yet military efforts to capture or kill terrorists are likely to be subordinate to measures to promote local participation in government and economic programs to spur development, as well as efforts to understand and address the grievances that often lie at the heart of insurgencies.[1]

> National Defense Strategy

In order to study two successful but relatively unknown counterinsurgencies conducted in the 20th century and compare these insurgencies to current United States counterinsurgency doctrine a researcher must not only understand FM 3-24, *Counterinsurgency*, but also the United States National Defense Strategy. The National Defense Strategy is only 23 pages long, but the doctrinal manual FM 3-24 is too detailed to be analyzed in its entirety within the context of this chapter. Although FM 3-24, *Counterinsurgency* is meant to be an all encompassing reference and one should not deliberately neglect analyses of any one part of the manual when conducting counterinsurgency operations, this study specifically focused on the principles and paradoxes of counterinsurgency referenced within the manual, as those principles apply to the case studies. Different sections of the manual correlate with other portions because many of the principles and paradoxes within a counterinsurgency intertwine during execution. Because some of the paradoxes support or fit within several of the principles, those paradoxes will be woven into the analysis of the principles. Within the principles, one has stood out as most important. The study of both Greece and Oman has shown that above all else within the counterinsurgency effort, legitimacy of the government is the most essential piece because it attacks what is really the center of gravity behind the insurgency--Ideology.[2] This principle will be covered in depth at the end of the chapter. But, before analyzing the specific doctrine of counterinsurgency, one must first understand exactly what doctrine is and what counterinsurgency means.

In defining doctrine in John Chamber's *American Military History,* Roger Spiller stated that theoretically military doctrines are dictated by military strategy which is derived from national strategy. He furthered his explanation by more appropriately arguing that in reality, doctrine results from differing schools of thought.[3] These schools of thought, in turn, come from the study of history. More specifically these schools of thought come from the analyses of successful and unsuccessful practices derived from similar warfare using similar weapon systems. What are deemed as successful practices and fit within the societal and cultural norms become the foundation for a nation's military doctrine. In fact, the American Army defines doctrine as –fundamental principles by which the military forces . . . guide their actions in support of national objectives." It further states that such doctrine is –authoritative but requires judgment in application."[4] Such historical examples do not have to be from a nation's own history to have an impact on doctrine. An example of this can be seen in the Army's AirLand Battle Doctrine that was developed after an intensive study of the Yom Kippur War in 1973. The study of the Arab-Israeli war showed lethality of conventional weapon systems with the understanding that such weapons were mutually supporting, and if fought individually were easily defeated. This combined with the understanding that

105

United States military forces were drastically outnumbered by the Soviet military combined to develop what became American doctrine from 1982 up through most of the 1990s until it was replaced by network-centric warfare. Now that doctrine is understood, one must understand the definition of the focus of this study--counterinsurgency.

The United States has been involved in many wars, but it labels only a few as counterinsurgencies. An insurgency is defined as "an organized movement aimed at the overthrow of a constituted government through the use of subversion and armed conflict."[5] Depending on which side of the fight one sits on, an insurgency can also be labeled a revolution or even in some cases a civil war. One could argue, especially taking the British perspective, that the American Revolution was an insurgency. Some would posit that although the American Indians were not insurgents Americans learned aspects of guerilla warfare from them. The years American Soldiers spent in the Philippines after the Spanish American War and again after World War II can be labeled as an insurgency. Vietnam is also an obvious example, because of its failures, that many naysayers compare to Iraq and Afghanistan to argue that America cannot win those wars.

Counterinsurgency refers to the United States political and military doctrine designed to defeat insurgencies influenced by the Soviet Union during the Cold War. But, counterinsurgencies have dated to at least as far back as the Napoleonic era. In fact, the term guerilla is Spanish for "little war" and is derived from the period 1808 to 1814 in which, despite their defeating nearly every army in Europe, the French were unable to subdue Spain. They lost over 250,000 casualties and eventually lost Spain.[6]

American doctrine specifically defines counterinsurgency as "those military, paramilitary, political, economic, psychological and civic actions taken by a government

106

to defeat an insurgency."[7] The term chosen to fight what Nikita Khrushchev labeled as

"wars of liberation" was counterinsurgency. Counterinsurgency was carefully chosen

instead of counterrevolutionary because of the "heroic connotations" many Americans

have come to associate with revolution, based off their own history.[8] With this logic

would Americans have to define the American Revolution as the American insurgency?

Does the very label of counterinsurgency detract from getting at the essential reasons for

the conflict? Interestingly enough, American military doctrinal manuals do not define

revolution. Webster's Dictionary defines revolution as "fundamental change in

political organization; especially the overthrow or renunciation of one government or

ruler and the substitution of another by the governed; activity or movement designed to

effect fundamental changes in the socio-economic situation."[9] With this definition, as

unpalatable as it might be to some for political reasons, one could begin to truly

understand the motivations behind the insurgent or revolutionary fighter. Once that is

understood then American Soldiers are in a better position to determine the center of

gravity--the ideology that causes those men to fight against the government, and they are

therefore better able understand how to use the principles outlined in FM 3-24 to gain

control of the conflict. Along with understanding the motivations behind why America's

enemies are fighting, American Soldiers must also understand the overall environment in

which they are fighting.

The enemy that the American Soldier fights in this type of conflict has a distinct

advantage. American doctrine states that in order to conduct successful

counterinsurgency operations, Soldiers and Marines must thoroughly understand the local

society and culture as well as the motivations, strengths and weaknesses of the enemy insurgent.[10] Oman offers a great example of the counterinsurgent advisor understanding the environment. The British advisors learned to work in concert with tribal practices and religious beliefs in order to motivate the indigenous fighters and recruit among the local population. They learned the best methods to conduct, what we today define as, information operations against the ideology of the Communist fighters they faced based off of local practices and technology available. The SAS fighting alongside the *Firqat* in the western Jebal quickly learned the terrain and exploited what advantages airpower offered while mitigating the advantages held by the *adoo*. They used the turned enemy fighters to help further exploit the weaknesses in the enemy supply capabilities. One way they were able to accomplish such a vast understanding of their environment, which is critical in counterinsurgency warfare, is to work hand-in-hand with the host national forces. This brings one to the next principle of American counterinsurgency doctrine.

The second major concept in the American counterinsurgency manual and one of the primary principles laid out in the doctrine is unity of effort. This concept is critical to the success in counterinsurgency operations; however despite the importance, American doctrine does not fully explain the different dimensions of its role. The focus on the manual is on unity of effort in regards to the civilian organizations and the host national government which are vital to success given that the center of gravity is not militarily achieved, but politically accomplished. The study in Greece best depicts the unity of effort that senior administration officials had concentrated on in dealing with the Greek Government. Unable to dictate exactly how the government should be run or the war fought, George McGhee, James Van Fleet, and Dwight Griswold, the senior American officials in Greece, had to persuade Greek officials including the Greek Prime Minister to change the government to a more representative and inclusive form.

The manual, however, fails to adequately address unity of effort in regard to the host national units. This lack of definition is evidenced by command charts made in Iraq within the last few years, charts that show Iraqi police and army units under United States Army brigade and division commands. Despite their efforts in diagramming the chain of command with Iraqi units being subordinate to American commanders, commanders in Iraq only succeeded in directing the Iraqi units to conduct missions that the Iraqis were interested in executing. In Oman, the British SAS learned that it needed to persuade the indigenous units and their leaders in order to accomplish certain missions. Understanding that indigenous forces must be persuaded, British officers focused on getting sheik, imam and governor approval to execute missions with the local forces. This additional step in Oman took indigenous forces well beyond the ambivalent nature displayed by many Iraqi police and military officers to a level of committed coalition partner. Having this most essential force allows for the counterinsurgent commander/advisor to better address another American principle of counterinsurgency warfare: Counterinsurgents should prepare for the long term commitment.

> Theory . . . demands that at the outset of war its character and scope should be determined on the basis of the political probabilities.[11]

Perhaps one of the most obvious but ultimately critical factors to be considered prior to conducting such wars is the length of time it takes to win an insurgency. The National Defense Strategy of June 2008 describes the current conflicts in Iraq and Afghanistan and the overall fight with Al-Qaeda and other violent extremist groups as part of the ―Long War.‖[12] Appendix A of FM 3-24, labeled ―A Guide for Action,‖ is divided into sections of "plan," "prepare," "execute" and "ending the tour" but does not

explain how to end the war. Instead, the appendix discusses an end of tour alluding to

continued years that United States forces will be utilized until victory is declared.[13]

When discussing the execution of conducting counterinsurgency operations, Sir Robert

Thompson is quoted in FM 3-24 on the British efforts in the successful Malayan

counterinsurgency, arguing that "there are no short-cuts and no gimmicks . . . that the

government must not allow itself to be diverted either by . . . the insurgent or by the

critics . . . who will be seeking a simpler and quicker solution."[14]

The wars in both Greece and Oman show that fighting a successful

counterinsurgency takes an extended period of time. Although America's involvement in

Greece's Civil War was from 1947 to 1949, the war began several years prior to U.S.

involvement. The disaffections which instigated the conflict could arguably date back

approximately fifteen years to when the Communist Party was outlawed and its political

members became underground dissidents. In Oman, the counterinsurgency lasted eleven

years, from 1964 to 1975, and was not the first insurgency that plagued Oman. Clashes

between the Imamate and the Sultan brought a similar warfare to northern Oman in the

1950s.[15] Both wars prove the principle of a counterinsurgency being a "long term

commitment."[16]

Understanding the importance of historical context in its role in development of

doctrine, one cannot exclude the results of the Vietnam War and how it played a part in

the American psyche and how it shapes future doctrine. One could argue that given

America's political four year cycle this principle plays an even more important role.

George Herring in his book *America's Longest War* explains that Richard Nixon won the presidential election in 1968 on a platform of ending the long drawn out war with an ‑honorable" finish.[17] The war had just lasted too long and American will had dwindled. Americans did not have the same vital interests at stake as they had in World War II and the final outcome was insufficiently important for Americans to stay in a protracted war that showed little progress.

This study's examples of successful counterinsurgency give a unique perspective to this phenomenon that is worth considering as America goes forward in what have already become long protracted wars in Afghanistan and Iraq. The type of force most effective in fighting a counterinsurgency, is not a large commitment of foreign forces, but a committed local force that knows the terrain, culture and enemy that it faces. This ties directly into the counterinsurgent principle of ‑use of appropriate force" and two paradoxes that intertwine with the principle. The paradox of counterinsurgencies that ‑sometimes the more force is used the less effective it is" supports the principle of appropriate force.[18] Another paradox that meshes with this concept is the idea that ‑the host nation doing something tolerably is normally better than [American Soldiers] doing it well."[19] These three ideas are illustrated in the Oman and Greece case studies.

Politicians in Britain and America faced similar issues in Oman and Greece. Both were secondary efforts. Great Britain's empire strained the country's resources after World War II. British troops were deployed to fight insurgencies in the British colonies of Palestine, Malaysia, and Kenya and the United Kingdom's military leadership was focused on Europe where there was fear of Soviet invasion. For that reason, Oman had limited British involvement in the conflict. Although the United States was not an imperial power like Britain it had its own reasons for wanting limited troop involvement.

With World War II just recently ending and occupation forces still deployed to Germany, Japan and the Philippines, America was unwilling to commit any ground troops to Greece despite the Greek government's request. The Truman administration committed only advisors at corps and higher level. In both counterinsurgencies, the force used consisted almost entirely of local nationals that were trained, equipped, and in the case of Oman led by British or American advisors. In neither case were large numbers of conventional troops deployed, avoiding the prospect of significant casualties that could have turned public will against the involvement.

America's national strategy document touches on this very point when it states that, ―Working with and through local actors whenever possible to confront common security challenges is the best and most sustainable approach to combat violent extremism."[20] This is paralleled in doctrine in one of the ―paradoxes" of counterinsurgency operations; ―The Host Nation Doing Something Tolerably is Normally Better than [Americans] Doing It Well."[21] In this paradox American counterinsurgency theorists have captured the understanding of establishing a host national force for the purposes of fighting the long war that is described in their national strategy, but the manual misses a critical point. It explains the host national forces within the framework of multinational forces, no doubt in order to provide legitimacy for the foreign efforts in the host country to the international community.[22] Instead, the manual should focus the host national force as the main effort not to provide international legitimacy, but more importantly, to provide legitimacy for those being governed. With the understanding that host national forces are essential in the makeup of military forces conducting counterinsurgency operations, the question then arises; what is the mission of those forces? The counterinsurgency principle of "security under the rule of law is essential" and the paradox, that "tactical success guarantees nothing" begin to answer this question and are well illustrated in the operations in Oman.[23]

Operations in the country show that the tactical fight, however important, will only set the conditions for the decisive operations in winning a counterinsurgency. The leadership within Oman understood this clearly and demonstrated it in their mission statement for the Dhofar Brigade. The brigade was "to secure Dhofar for civilian development."[24] This allowed for the British and the Sultan to focus on the real center of gravity--the motivation or ideology behind the insurgency. Another important lesson brought out by the Dhofar example is mentioned in the paradox to counterinsurgency; "Many important decisions are not made by generals" which supports the principle of "empower the lowest levels."[25] Taken a step further this supports the premise of civilian leadership. The Dhofar Development Committee, run by the governor of the Dhofar region approved the military campaigns, not the senior British general. Leadership of the counterinsurgency effort led by the civilian leadership not only allowed for the "unity of effort" described within FM 3-24, it more importantly established the perception of legitimacy, in that the government had been improving and securing the lives of the people of Dhofar. This attacked the real center of gravity of the insurgency.

Counterinsurgency states very clearly that the center of gravity is usually the insurgency's "ability to generate and sustain popular support, or at least acquiescence and tolerance."[26] This definition does not get at the very root of the problem. If taken for its literal definition, the doctrine states that killing a charismatic leader, destroying a radio or phone system, shutting down a newspaper, or blocking emails and websites could theoretically be enough to effectively defeat the insurgent.

If the counterinsurgent force attacks one method of communication, and the idea is legitimate and the grievance worth fighting for, then even if the method of garnering support was disabled, a determined ideologically driven insurgent, will find another way to get the narrative out. It is analogous to a weapons factory that utilizes multiple roads, rivers, airports and railroads to ship its weapons to the front. If you attack the railroad, then the enemy will use the roads, and if the roads, the enemy will revert to the rivers and if the rivers the enemy can revert to airdrop. How can such ―abilities" be the center of gravity? In fact, they are not. The center of gravity is the weapon, and to the insurgent the idea is that weapon. The idea is the grievance, which FM 3-24 even states is how ―many insurgencies begin because groups within a society believe that they have been denied political rights."[27] The question is, then, why does the American military not just make the fighting the idea central to its counterinsurgency doctrine? Although it discusses the ideas, transmitted through narrative as being ―the motivating factor in insurgent activity," it does not make this ideology the center of gravity.[28] After all doctrine is in the very simplest definition a belief or principle that is taught.[29] If legitimate representative rule is a fundamental idea within American values and the primary explanation of U.S. involvement, then why not make it part of its counterinsurgency doctrine? As far back as Harry S. Truman and America's involvement in Greece to as recently as George W. Bush and Iraq, American political leadership has explained the reasons for involvement in such conflicts as ideological. American doctrine should indentify that goal as the primary reason for conducting counterinsurgency operations. The purpose and end state would then be understood and would positively affect future operations. If the idea of legitimate representative government is the true center of gravity, then this places the military in a supporting role to the State Department, led by the ambassador.

Focusing on this objective attacks the insurgent's own ideology. Chapter one of *Counterinsurgency* states that ―ideas are the motivating factor in insurgent activities."[30] In Oman, once Sultan Qaboos gained legitimacy through his efforts to rebuild the Dhofar region and bring prosperity to the area, the ideas that initially motivated the insurgents were no longer valid. This proves yet another part of the counterinsurgency doctrine accurate, in that the best weapon in Oman ―for counterinsurgency [did] not shoot."[31] Recent scholarship supports this conclusion.

In 2008, Robert Jones in the *Small Wars Journal* stated that focus defeating the violent extremist organization forces the military to attack the symptom as opposed to the problem. He then urged his audience to move their national strategy toward a populace-centric engagement, by focusing on the sickness or the environment instead of the symptom, the insurgent.[32] Indeed, this study found that successful counterinsurgencies did just that. The military is analogous to the headache medicine, which should be prescribed to control the symptoms while the State Department, Non Governmental Organizations (NGOs) and specific smaller elements of the military focus on the causes or the operational environment that allowed for those extremists to exist.

Although Jones defends his thesis by giving positive examples on a much larger world stage, this same concept can be tied to a more definitive operational level of war during a successful counterinsurgency. Indeed in Dhofar, the government worked on

115

treating the sickness and the military focused on preventing the fever or enemy from getting worse until the sickness could be cured. The military maintained defense of the region for the sole purpose of allowing economic growth and stability. If the sickness remained, whatever the problems were, the symptoms would continue to return.

The nature of bureaucratic survival means that such organizations are always trying to expand, not give up powers to another bureaucracy. If the United States military is willing to reject this aspect, and ultimate weakness of bureaucracy, then it would agree that it should not have the lead in any counterinsurgency. It should be an enabling force to a political lead. Clausewitz's time honored precept that —war is only a branch of political activity; that it is in no sense autonomous . . . [and] simply continuation of political intercourse, with addition of other means" is still valid.[33] Yet, today, who is the central figure reporting to Congress on the war in Iraq or Afghanistan? Not the ambassador or the Secretary of State, but the Multi-National Force (MNF) Commander or Central Command (CENTCOM) Commander. The face that everyone in America ties to the war on terror is not Hillary Clinton, nor Ambassador David Crocker, but General David Petraeus. Some might argue that this might be perception and not reality, but if one looks at who controls the largest amounts of money and equipment invested into the Iraqi economy and military one can clearly see that the CENTCOM Commander, not the ambassador, is indeed the central figure. FM 3-24, typical of a document created by a bureaucracy, does not make that point clear and in fact, when discussing other agencies, it describes coordination instead of subordination.

FM 3-24 begins the chapter on —Unity of Effort" with a subtitle---—Integrating Civilian and Military Activities."[34] Immediately below the title to the chapter is a

116

quotation from David Galula's *Counterinsurgency Warfare* that explains that the military

action during counterinsurgency operations -is second to the political one, its primary

purpose being to afford enough freedom" and safety for the political piece to have a

chance at success.[35] The chapter explains the inherent complexities and reason why it is

important to limit or erase the violence within the contested region, labeling it as a -key

aspect" in the struggle.[36] The chapter does not, however, make it clear that the military

forces within the region should be subordinated to a political leader, but this study has

shown that such subordination works. With ideology understood as the center of gravity

and military subordination to legitimate representative government inherent in

counterinsurgency operations one can come to the last principle of counterinsurgency this

study has analyzed.

      Counterinsurgency states that -insurgents must be isolated from their cause and

support."[37] It explains that it is -easier to separate an insurgency from its resources and

let it die than to kill every insurgent."[38] In neither Oman nor Greece were all the

insurgents killed. In both Oman and Greece the ruling governments offered periods of

amnesty that had possibly an even greater effect than killing the insurgents. As American

counterinsurgency doctrine explains that such lethal operations might in fact create

further resentment. In most cases an insurgent killed is a brother, father, husband or

cousin to locals and his death, even if justified, causes resentment and will possibly sway

others to join the fight. However, especially in the case of Oman, such periods of

amnesty were decisive in limiting manpower for the insurgent force, creating popular

ideological shift to support the government within the region, and providing a critical

capability or intelligence asset to attack the hard core insurgents that refuse to abandon their fight. Once this ideological separation of the insurgent from the local populace took place in Oman and Greece, the military forces in both countries conducted the easier physical separation between the insurgent and outside support.

Oman and Greece therefore serve as examples of successful counterinsurgencies that support the principles and paradoxes of American counterinsurgency doctrine. However, they also demonstrate that the current leadership structure with which America conducts such operations is flawed. Analyses of these two obscure, but successful counterinsurgencies identify a need for a shift in leadership from the military commander to the political chief. Additionally, examinations of these conflicts show that the counterinsurgency model should have a more focused examination of the ideological motivation behind the insurgency and treat that motivation as the insurgent center of gravity. In conclusion, both counterinsurgencies, through understanding the ideological center of gravity and attacking it in a non-lethal approach, supported by military actions, proved effective in defeating the insurgent forces within their border.

---

[1] "National Defense Strategy," Department of Defense, ed., (June 2008), 23, 8.

[2] Department of the Army, *Field Manual 3-24, Counterinsurgency* (Washington, DC: Government Printing Office, 2006),1-75.

[3] Roger Spiller, "Military Doctrine", John Whiteclay Chambers II, ed., *American Military History* (Oxford: Oxford University Press, 1999), 231-232.

[4] Department of the Army, *Field Manual 1-02, Operational Terms and Graphics* (Washington, DC: Government Printing Office, 2004),1-65.

[5] Ibid., 1-101.

[6] David G. Chandler, *Dictionary of Napoleonic Wars* (New York: Macmillan Publishing, 1979), 187-188.

[7] *Operational Terms and Graphics,* 1-47.

[8]John Whiteclay Chambers II, *American Military History* (Oxford: Oxford University Press, 1999), 189.

[9]—Merriam-Webster's Collegiate Dictionary," Frederick C. Mish, ed., *Merriam-Webster's Collegiate Dictionary* (Springfield: Merriam-Webster, Inc., 2003), 1068.

[10]*Counterinsurgency,* 1-22 - 1-23.

[11]Carl von Clausewitz, *On War* (New York: Alfred A. Knopf, 1993), 706.

[12]—National Defense Strategy," 7.

[13]—Merriam-Webster's Collegiate Dictionary," A-9.

[14]Ibid., 5-1. Originally, Sir Robert Thompson, *Defeating Communist Insurgency: The Lessons of Malaya and Vietnam* (New York: Praeger, 1966).

[15]J. E. Peterson, *Oman's Insurgencies: The Sultanate's Struggles for Supremacy* (London: SAQI Books, 2007), 66-67.

[16]*Counterinsurgency*, 1-24.

[17]George C. Herring, *America's Longest War: The United States and Vietnam, 1950-1975* (New York: Alfred A. Knopf,1979), 221-224.

[18]*Counterinsurgency*, 1-25, 1-27.

[19]Ibid.

[20]—National Defense Strategy." 8.

[21]*Counterinsurgency*, 1-27.

[22]Ibid., 2-4.

[23]Ibid., 1-23, 1-28.

[24]Ian Gardiner, *In the Service of the Sultan: A First Hand Account of the Dhofar Insurgenc,* (South Yorkshire, England: 2007), 72-73.

[25]Department of the Army, *Field Manual 3-24, Counterinsurgency* (Washington, DC: Government Printing Office, 2006), 1-28.

[26]Ibid., 3-13.

[27]Ibid., 3-12.

[28]Ibid., 1-14.

[29] "Merriam-Webster's Collegiate Dictionary", 368.

[30] Department of the Army, *Field Manual 3-24, Counterinsurgency* (Washington, DC: Government Printing Office, 2006), 114.

[31] Ibid., 1-27.

[32] Robert C. Jones, *Winning the Ideological Battle for the Support of the Populace (Understanding the Role of Ideology in Insurgency)*, (*Small Wars Journal*, Volume 10, April 13, 2008).

[33] Clausewitz, *On War*, 731.

[34] *Counterinsurgency*, i, 2-1.

[35] Ibid., 2-1.

[36] Ibid.

[37] Ibid., 1-23.

[38] Ibid.

CHAPTER 5

CONCLUSIONS AND RECOMMENDATIONS

The events of September 11, 2001, brought America into a long-term struggle that will stretch its diplomatic, military and economic resources comparably beyond any conflict except World War II. Compounding this fact, the past eight years have already proven this military aspect of the struggle will not end in a decisive battle as did Desert Storm in 1990. Instead, success will be determined in far less dramatic ways which have not yet been fully explained. As critical resources become more finite and the information revolution fans different ideology, conflict will inevitably follow. Given America's position as superpower and its penchant for providing assistance and security around the globe it will continue to combat extremism around the world. It simply does not have the manpower, economy or will to fight on so many fronts for such extended periods of time. In order to adjust to these limitations America must adapt its approaches and set a clear end state for success. To do that it must rely more on local national forces which have the added benefit of demonstrating legitimacy for the government. America's military must train, equip and assist these forces with the understanding that they are enablers to the decisive operation in counterinsurgencies, which is the establishment of a stable, legitimate, and in most cases a representative form of government. This will not be easy.

America's enemies have adapted. They have learned that they do not have the ability to stand and fight in a conventional battle against the American military, so they have switched strategies. America's enemies in the Middle East have studied history and learned a doctrinal approach to fight a more powerful enemy from Mao Tse-tung and others. They are now attacking the center of gravity of the American military-the American will to fight. It is the Achilles heel of the powerful American military and the wound has been exploited once so far in the 20th century for all of its enemies to see. Extremist organizations such as Al Qaeda in Iraq and the Taliban in Afghanistan have most likely learned from the Vietnam experience that a war of exhaustion properly executed can defeat America's premier military not through tactical success, but long term strategic exhaustion. Efforts against the Soviet Army in Afghanistan proved that perseverance, determination and constant adaptation can win out over technologically superior conventional force. So, in order to defeat them, America's military must adapt too.

Initial efforts in the form of FM 3-24 are a step in the right direction. The American counterinsurgency doctrinal manual has been lauded by America's allies in Great Britain and has shown some success in Iraq. The manual uses historical examples and cites many counterinsurgency experts throughout its pages. Its foundation has been solidly laid within historical examples and its assumptions on how to fight a counterinsurgency appear valid. Yet, the military practitioner who relinquishes the constant effort to adapt and improve on his profession is bound to surrender the initiative to his enemy. For that reason, this study has examined the principles and paradoxes of FM 3-24, *Counterinsurgency* in comparison to the counterinsurgency efforts of the British in Oman and the Americans in Greece and has determined the beliefs it advocates, are valid.

Through the study of Greece and Oman we gain invaluable insight concerning to what principles, characteristics, force make up, and end-state have been successfully executed to win the counterinsurgency fight. One can literally take those experiences from previous soldiers and learn from them without having actually experienced combat. In the case of these two conflicts a professional soldier can, without spending years climbing the Jebal or slogging through the mountainous terrain of west Macedonia, learn how a successful, yet limited counterinsurgency was fought. He can also learn how soldiers in those experiences were able to adapt faster than the enemy and win in a highly fluid environment.

Based on the results of the Oman study it can be clearly seen that when quality people are in advisory and leadership positions, they are very effective in training local forces and conducting missions against the insurgents. In order to assure that these individuals have the right temperament, desire, expertise, courage and natural leadership abilities, they must be strictly selected. The British provided support, equipment, money and oversight to develop host nation security forces. Understanding their primary mission was not to kill or capture the enemy, but to provide security for the political and economic reforms the government provided, these selected experts walked a suitable line between killing the hardcore *Adoo* and winning the hearts and minds of the inhabitants. Through their leadership and experience they effectively advised both the Sultan's armed forces and the locally raised *Firqat* and those units were very effective against the enemy forces. Senior leadership focused on affecting administrative and political decisions within the government while brigade and below leadership was tied directly into civilian control. Instead of being liaisons used to give orders to host national forces they were truly embedded with the host national forces.

This study of both the Greek Civil War and the Oman insurgency has both validated and provided the impetus of criticism in regards to the current American military counterinsurgency doctrine. One could argue almost every paradox or aspect mentioned in FM 3-24 somehow is showcased or demonstrated in those two small and relatively unknown wars. However, the manual that defines the way we fight counterinsurgencies fails to properly identify the center of gravity of the insurgent or the intent behind why we fight that type of war. This thesis has illustrated the importance of our Soldiers and Marines understanding not only the paradoxes and the imperatives of a counterinsurgency but the overarching reason of why we as American Soldiers and Marines are deployed within that environment.

Unlike wars against competing nation states, insurgencies are primarily fought over legitimate governance. The disaffected inhabitants, if not given proper redress to fix their problems, will attempt to change that government if necessary by insurgent warfare. Understanding that it is principally ideology expressed through insurgent narrative that motivates that insurgency we can identify the true center of gravity of the insurgent. It is not limited to just how the insurgent builds support within the country, but more importantly the idea behind why he fights.

Above all, the counterinsurgencies in Oman and Greece have shown the overarching importance of identifying Ideology as the center of gravity. Both wars illustrate the need for political stability within the nation. In improving the perception of government legitimacy, both countries attacked the very center of gravity of the insurgent forces. By a surprising twist of fate, President Harry S. Truman's public relations people were able to persuade the chief decision makers within the Truman administration on

124

how to sell the war to the American people. The United States showed it supported the

Greek government in an attempt to preserve democracy, and a very fortuitous byproduct

occurred. In order to fit within the public expectations, the United States had to be

supporting a moderate representative government and therefore behind the scenes its

advisors and representatives pushed, prodded and cajoled the Greek government to adopt

a more representative government that allowed for the full spectrum of Greek citizens to

be represented. Greece understood the necessity of American support and became a more

representative government. The extreme ideology of the Greek Communists lost the

ability to sway the more moderate Greeks and support dwindled. Unable to rely on

Yugoslavian support and no longer having the support of the populace, the Communists

were unable to adequately fight against the government forces.

Similarly in Oman, after the Sultan Qaboos overthrew his father and began

significant land, economic and technological reform for the Dhofar region, the extreme

ideology that initially fueled the Jebalis in Dhofar no longer appealed to the average

Adoo. More importantly, Jebalis now saw the atheist and extremist ideology of the

Communist insurgents as more of a danger than that of their Sultan. The amnesty

program that the Sultan instituted exploited this new weakness and the Communist

insurgents lost their support from within Dhofar. This accomplished, the much easier

physical task of separating the insurgents from their support from Yemen could be

completed by military forces cutting the lines of communication along the border of

Yemen and Oman.

In the final analysis, American military counterinsurgency doctrine detailed in

FM 3-24, *Counterinsurgency* addresses most lessons learned from countering insurgency within Greece and Oman. However, this study shows one inherent weakness that if not fixed could lead to confusion. The manual tells American troops how to get to the objective and what the right things to do on the objective might look like, but fails to tell them the most important part of any operations order. Why are they doing it? What is the overall big picture? What is the commander's intent? Today, the American Soldier is a professional who if given the full picture, will use historical analyses, an understanding of the contemporary environment in which he is are fighting in and the overall intent to adapt and accomplish any mission. Without all those factors being understood, they will continue in what can best be described as a counterinsurgency —fog of war."

In order to do this, American doctrine writers should redraft FM 3-24 slightly, adapting the sections dealing with unity of effort to address the explanation of persuasion that is inherit in dealing with local national forces as opposed to the unity of command that of which Soldiers are familiar. It must also shift its focus and label insurgent ideology and motivation in what it describes as the insurgent narrative as the center of gravity, and it must explain that in order to best attack that ideology the American military becomes an enabling effort to the decisive State Department role in developing a legitimate, representative, moderate and stable government.

TIMELINE--GREECE

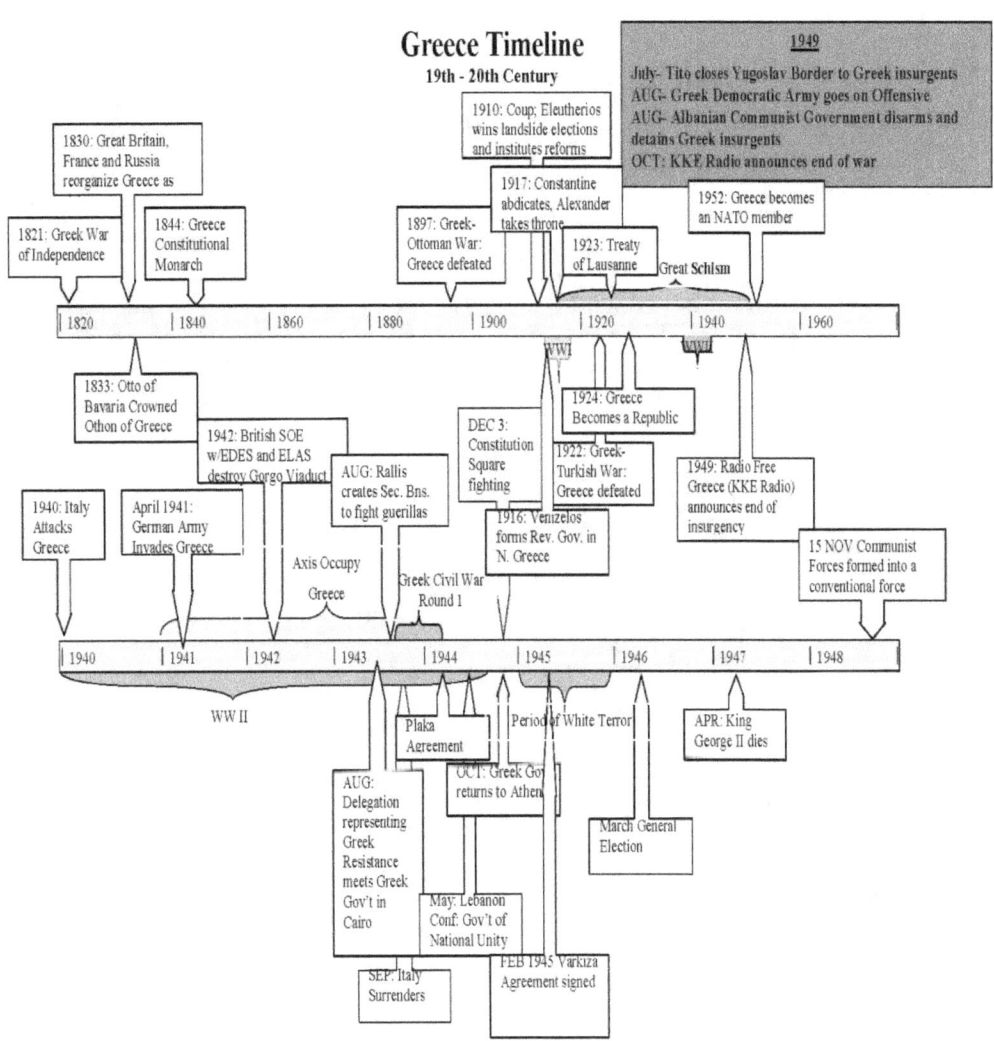

Greece Timeline
19th - 20th Century

1949
July- Tito closes Yugoslav Border to Greek insurgents
AUG- Greek Democratic Army goes on Offensive.
AUG- Albanian Communist Government disarms and detains Greek insurgents
OCT: KKE Radio announces end of war

1830: Great Britain, France and Russia reorganize Greece as

1910: Coup; Eleutherios wins landslide elections and institutes reforms

1821: Greek War of Independence

1844: Greece Constitutional Monarch

1897: Greek-Ottoman War: Greece defeated

1917: Constantine abdicates, Alexander takes throne

1923: Treaty of Lausanne

Great Schism

1952: Greece becomes an NATO member

| 1820 | 1840 | 1860 | 1880 | 1900 | 1920 | 1940 | 1960 |

WWI

WWII

1833: Otto of Bavaria Crowned Othon of Greece

1942: British SOE w/EDES and ELAS destroy Gorgo Viaduct

AUG: Rallis creates Sec. Bns. to fight guerillas

DEC 3: Constitution Square fighting

1924: Greece Becomes a Republic

1922: Greek-Turkish War: Greece defeated

1949: Radio Free Greece (KKE Radio) announces end of insurgency

1940: Italy Attacks Greece

April 1941: German Army Invades Greece

Axis Occupy Greece

Greek Civil War Round 1

1916: Venizelos forms Rev. Gov. in N. Greece

15 NOV Communist Forces formed into a conventional force

| 1940 | 1941 | 1942 | 1943 | 1944 | 1945 | 1946 | 1947 | 1948 |

WW II

Plaka Agreement

Period of White Terror

APR: King George II dies

AUG: Delegation representing Greek Resistance meets Greek Gov't in Cairo

OCT: Greek Gov returns to Athen

March General Election

May: Lebanon Conf: Gov't of National Unity

SEP: Italy Surrenders

FEB 1945 Varkiza Agreement signed

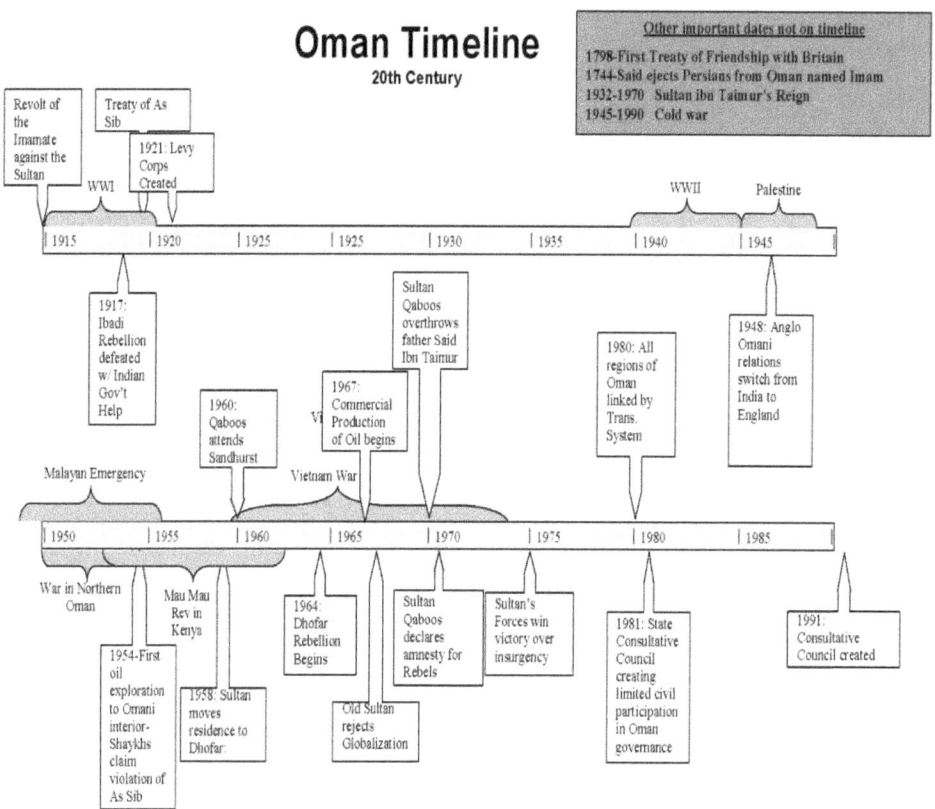

Oman Timeline
20th Century

Other important dates not on timeline
1798-First Treaty of Friendship with Britain
1744-Said ejects Persians from Oman named Imam
1932-1970 Sultan ibn Taimur's Reign
1945-1990 Cold war

BIBLIOGRAPHY

Akehurst, John. *We Won a War: The Campaign in Oman 1965-1975*. Southhampton: Michael Russell, 1982.

Aslanis, Eugen J. ―Guerrilla War in Greece: 1946-1949." The Command and General Staff College, 1968.

Barnett, Thomas P.M. *The Pentagon's New Map: War and Peace in the Twenty-First Century*. New York: G. P. Putnam's Sons, 2004.

Beckett, Ian F. W. ―Insurgency in Iraq: An Historical Perspective." Carlisle: PA: Department of Defense, 2005.

Birtle, Andrew J. *U.S. Army Counterinsurgency and Contingency Operations Doctrine: 1942-1976*. Washington, DC: Center of Military History, 2007.

Blaufarb, Douglas. *The Counterinsurgency Era: U.S. Doctrine and Performance, 1950 to the Present*. New York: Free Press, 1977.

Burks, R. V. ―Statistical Profile of Greek Communist." *Journal of Modern History* 27 no. No. 2 (1955): 153-58.

Cable, Larry. *Conflict of Myths: The Development of American Counterinsurgency Doctrine and the Vietnam War*. New York: New York University Press, 1986.

Calwell, Charles E. *Small Wars: Their Principles and Practice*. Lincoln, NE: : University of Nebraska Press, 1996. Reprint, Small Wars: A Tactical Textbook for Imperial Soldiers 1890.

Chambers II, John Whiteclay *American Military History*. Oxford: Oxford University Press, 1999.

Chandler, David G. *Dictionary of Napoleonic Wars*. New York: Macmillan Publishing, 1979.

Clausewitz, Carl von. *On War*. Translated by Michael Howard and Peter Paret. 13 ed. New York: Alfred A. Knopf, 1993.

Clogg, Richard. *A Concise History of Greece*. Cambridge: Cambridge University Press, 1992.

―――. *A Short History of Modern Greece*. Cambridge: Cambridge University Press, 1979.

Clutterbuck, Richard. *The Long, Long War: Counterinsurgency in Malaya and Vietnam*. New York: Frederick A. Praeger, 1966.

Condit, D.M. et al. *A Counterinsurgency Bibliography*. Washington, DC: American University, Special Operations Research Office, 1963.

Corum, James S. *Bad Strategies*. First ed. Minneapolis, MN: Zenith Press, 2008.

Curtis, Glenn E. *Greece: A Country Study*. 4th ed, *Country Studies*. Washington, DC: Department of the Army, 1995.

Department of the Army. Field Manual 1-02, *Operational Terms and Graphics*. Washington, DC: Government Printing Office, 2004.

———. Field Manual 3-24, *Counterinsurgency*. Washington, DC: Government Printing Office, 2006.

Department of Defense. *National Defense Strategy*. Washington, DC: Government Printing office, 2008.

DePauw, John and George Luz, eds. *Winning the Peace: The Strategic Implications of Military Civic Action*. Carlisle Barracks, PA: Strategic Studies Institute, 1990.

Galula, David. *Counter-Insurgency Warfare: Theory and Practice*. New York: Frederick A. Praeger, 1964.

Gardiner, Ian. *In the Service of the Sultan: A First Hand Account of the Dhofar Insurgency*. South Yorkshire, England: Pen & Sword Books, 2007.

Gerolymatos, Andre. *Red Acropolis, Black Terror: The Greek Civil War and the Origins of Soviet-American Rivalry, 1943-1949*. New York: Basic Books, 2004.

Gleason, S. Everett. ―Foreign Relations of the United States, 1947: The near East and Africa." edited by U.S. Department of State: Government Printing Press, 1973.

Gurr, Ted Robert. *Why Men Rebel*. Princeton, NJ: Princeton University Press, 1971.

Hammes, T. X. *The Sling and the Stone*. Osceola, WI: Zenith Press, 2004.

Herring, George C. *America's Longest War: The United States and Vietnam, 1950-1975*. New York: Alfred A. Knopf, 1979.

Hoffman, Valerie J. ―Ibadi Islam: An Introduction." 2009.

Howe, Stephen F. ―Fighting the Global War on Terro Tolerably: Augmenting the Global Counter Insurgency Strategy with Surrogates." Monograph, United States Army Command and General Staff College, 2007.

Hunt, Julian Ewell and Ira. *Sharpening the Combat Edge: The Use of Analysis to Reinforce Military Judgement*. Washington, DC: Department of the Army, 1974.

Iatrides, John O. ―Greece at the Crossroads, 1944-1950." In *Greece at the Crossroads: The Civil War and Its Legacy*, edited by John O. Iatrides and Linda Wrigley, 1-30. University Park: Penns.: The Pennsylvania State University Press, 1995.

Jeapes, Tony. *Sas: Operation Oman*. Vol. 4. Nashville, TN: The Battery Press, Inc., 1980.

Jones, Howard. *A New Kind of War: America's Global Strategy and the Truman Doctrine in Greece*. Oxford: Oxford University Press, 1989.

Jones, Robert. ―Winning the Ideological Battle for the Support of the Populace," *Small Wars Journal* Vol 10 April 13, 2008.

―――. ―Truman Doctrine." In *The Oxford Companion to American Military History*, edited by John Whiteclay Chambers II. Oxford: Oxford University Press, 1999.

Keegan, John. *The Face of Battle*. London: Penguin Books, 1976.

―――. *The Second World War*. New York: Penguin Books, 1990.

Kiste, Jon Van der. *Kings of the Hellenes*. Gloucestershire: Alan Sutton Publishing, 1994.

Kitson, Frank. *Low Intensity Operations: Subversion, Insurgency, Peace-Keeping*. Harrisburg, Pa:: Stackpole Books, 1971.

Kourvetaris, George Andrew. ―Professional Self-Images and Political Perspectives in the Greek Military." *American Sociological Review* 36, no. December (1971): 1043-57.

Kousoulas, D. George. *Revolution and Defeat*. London: Oxford University Press, 1965.

Kousoulas, Dimitrios G. *The Price of Freedom*. Syracuse: Syracuse University Press, 1953.

M. A. Campbell, E. W. Downs, and L. V. Schuetta. ―The Employment of Airpower in the Greek Guerilla War, 1947-1949." In *Air Studies*, edited by Concepts Division U.S. Aerospace Studies Institute: Air University, 1964.

Machiavelli, Niccolo. *The Prince*. Fort Wayne; IN: Sweetwater Press, 2006.

McCuen, John J. *The Art of Counter-Revolutionary War: The Strategy of Counter-Insurgency*. Harrisburg: Stackpole Books, 1966.

Melamid, Alexander. ―Dhofar." *Geographical Review* 74 no. 1, no. JAN 1984 (1984): 106-09.

Merom, Gil. *How Democracies Lose Small Wars: State, Society, and the Failures of France in Algeria, Israel in Lebanon, and the United States in Vietnam.* New York: Cambridge University Press, 2003.

—Merriam-Webster's Collegiate Dictionary." In *Merriam-Webster's Collegiate Dictionary*, edited by Frederick C. Mish. Springfield: Mass.: Merriam-Webster, Inc., 2003.

Metz, Helen Chapin, ed. *Turkey: A Country Study.* 5th ed, *Country Studies*: Department of the Army, 1995.

O'Ballance, Edgar. *The Greek Civil War, 1944-1949.* New York: Frederick A. Praeger, 1966.

Oman, Sultanate of. http://www.Omanet.Om/English/Regions/Dhofar.Asp?Cat=Reg Ministry of Information of Oman, 2009 http://www.omanet.com/english/regions/dhofar.asp?cat=reg. (accessed May 22 2009 2009).

Paget, Julian. *Counter-Insurgency Operations: Techniques of Guerilla Warfare.* New York: Walker and Company, 1967.

Persian Gulf States. Edited by Helen Chapin Metz. 3rd Edition ed, *Country Study.* Washington, DC: Department of the Army, 1994.

Peters, Ralph. *Fighting for the Future: Will America Triumph?* 1st ed. Mechanicsburg: PA: Stackpole Books, 1999.

Peterson, J. E. *Oman's Insurgencies: The Sultanate's Struggles for Supremacy.* London: SAQI Books, 2007.

Pribbenow, Merle L. *Victory in Vietnam: The Official History of the People's Army of Vietnam, 1954-1975.* Translated by Merle Pribbenow. Lawrence, KS: University Press of Kansas, 2002.

Sepp, Kalev I. —Best Practices in Counterinsurgency." *Military Review* 85 (2005): 8-12.

Shy, John. —The Military Conflict Considered as a Revolutionary War." In *Essays on the American Revolution*, H301RA-25 - H01RA-41. Fort Leavenworth, KS: USACGSC, DEC 2008. Reprint, H300: Roots of Today's Operational Environment.

Smith, Walter Bedell. —Letter to Secretary of State." edited by U.S. Department of State. Washington, DC: US Government Printing Office, January 8, 1947.

Spiller, Roger. —Military Doctrine." In *American Military History.* Edited by John Whiteclay Chambers II. Oxford: Oxford University Press, 1999.

Stavrakis, Peter J. *Moscow and Greek Communism, 1944-1949*. Ithaca, N.Y.: Cornell University Press, 1989.

Taber, Robert. *War of the Flea: The Classic Study of Guerilla Warfare*. Dulles, VA: Potomac Books, 2002.

Thompson, Robert, ed. *War in Peace: Conventional and Guerrilla Warfare since 1945*. 1st ed. New York: Harmony Books, 1981.

Thompson, Sir Robert. *Defeating Communist Insurgency: The Lessons of Malaya and Vietnam, Studies in International Security*. New York: Praeger, 1966.

Vlavianos, Haris. *Greece, 1941-49: From Resistance to Civil War*. New York: St. Martin's Press, 1992.

Weinberg, Gerhard L. *A World at Arms: A Global History of World War II*. Cambridge: Cambridge University Press, 1994.

Wittner, Lawrence S. *American Intervention in Greece, 1943-1949*. Edited by William E. Leuchtenburg, *Contemporary American History Series*. New York: Columbia University Press, 1982.

Zotos, Stephanos. *Greece: The Struggle for Freedom*. New York: Thomas Y. Cromwell Company, 1967.